Nurturing Children and Families:

One Model of a Parent/Child Program in a Waldorf School

Sarah Baldwin

SECOND EDITION

WECAN
WALDORF EARLY CHILDHOOD
ASSOCIATION OF NORTH AMERICA

Editor: Susan Howard
Managing Editors: Lydia Roberson and Lory Widmer
Layout and Design: Sheila Harrington
Text Editing: Sandy Milczarek
Administrative Support: Melissa Lyons and Melissa Farrell McDonagh

This publication was made possible by a grant from the Waldorf Curriculum Fund.

Published in the United States
by the Waldorf Early Childhood Association of North America
285 Hungry Hollow Road
Spring Valley, NY 10977
845-352-1690
info@waldorfearlychildhood.org
www.waldorfearlychildhood.org

ISBN
978-1-936849-25-3

Acknowledgments

*T*here are many gifted and talented teachers who have been doing parent/child work much longer than I. Some of them have been a great source of inspiration to me, and I am grateful for the sharing of their wisdom and for what I have learned from them. Cynthia Aldinger, Jill Bieber, Louise de Forest, Connie Manson, Rena Osmer, Susan Silverio and Connie White have all shared freely with me their insights, intuition and inspiration. I have benefited greatly from the fruit of their life's work as they helped the teacher in me to take shape. I am also indebted to my colleagues at Ashwood Waldorf School for their support and for giving me the freedom, space and resources to create something new out of my own imagination.

Special thanks must be given to Susan Howard, who recognized the need for this book and was enthusiastic about its publication before it was even written—having faith that I would produce something worthy of publication; to Susan Weber for her support and for finding a quiet moment amidst the many demands on her time to write a beautiful preface; to Lydia Roberson, of WECAN Publications, for helping to tie up all of the loose ends; and especially to Nancy Foster, for not only carefully reading the manuscript, offering excellent editorial advice and complimentary words in her foreword; but also, and most importantly, for persisting in nudging this project forward toward its final end.

Much love and affection go to my two wonderful sons, Harper and Whit, who led me to Waldorf education in the first place, and to my hardworking husband and proofreader, Max—all who sacrificed wife and mommy time in order to allow me to complete this project. Thanks, too, to Laura for her friendship, support and patient listening.

But my deepest gratitude goes to the parents and families who have participated in my parent/child classes at Ashwood. They have helped me to grow as a teacher, and their presence in my life has enriched it immeasurably. This book would not exist without them.

Table of Contents

Editor's Note

*T*wenty years ago, parent/child classes were a rarity in Waldorf communities. Many parents discovered the riches of Waldorf early childhood education only when their child turned three or four and began to attend the nursery-kindergarten. "If we had only known about all of this a few years earlier!" they often said. As a response, Waldorf early childhood educators began to develop classes for parents and toddlers; today such groups and programs exist in nearly every Waldorf school community. Known as Parent/Child or Parent/Toddler or Parent/Infant classes, or as Mommie-and-Me, Mothers-and-Tots or even Cricket-on-the-Hearth, they have become a tremendous source of support for parenting and early childhood education in our communities.

In the past ten years, this work has fully established itself, and Waldorf grade school teachers often comment on the strong foundations they experience in both the children and the families who have participated in these classes. The parent/child class experience can be life-changing for both parent and child, strengthening a spirit of openness and joy in development, and creating opportunities for community-building in times where parenting can be a somewhat isolated and even lonely experience.

This publication began as a Master's degree project during Sarah Baldwin's Waldorf early childhood studies at Sunbridge College. After completing her training, Sarah went on to lead Parent/Child classes at the Ashwood School in Maine, and to consult with other colleagues who have been pioneers in this work.

The Waldorf Early Childhood Association is pleased to offer this new edition of Sarah Baldwin's book. Further publications on parent/child classes are also planned for the near future. We hope that these resources will stimulate the further development of this important work on behalf of very young children and the families who love and care for them.

Susan Howard, WECAN Coordinator

Foreword

When I began parent/child work at Acorn Hill Waldorf Kindergarten and Nursery after many years there as a kindergarten teacher, I felt, along with eagerness for a new challenge, a bit of trepidation about entering this completely new realm. Not only would I be working with much younger children—two-and-a-half to three-year-olds instead of four- to six-year-olds—but the parents would also be part of the class.

It was my good fortune, thus, to take up the work first as an apprentice with my colleague Cecelia Karpoff, one of the pioneers in the parent/child field. What a gift it was to begin by learning through imitation and experience, just like a young child, and to grow into the work with the guidance of an experienced mentor.

Perhaps nothing can equal the experience of working with a gifted mentor. In reading Sarah Baldwin's manuscript for the first time, however, I felt that this book would be the best possible substitute for such a mentorship. Sarah's writing is clear, yet warm and welcoming in tone. She offers wise counsel based on her own experience, with a sense of honesty, good humor, and humility that is refreshing and inspires confidence. Along with helpful clarity, the reader receives the all-important sense of being left free to find his or her own way. Sarah never gives the idea that she has found "the right approach," only that she has found a way that has been successful in her particular situation.

Now, ten years after the first publication of Sarah's book, I am no longer teaching, but I can still remember how healing it was for the parents in my class to experience the daily rhythm of in-breath and out-breath, and to discover that their engagement in purposeful "household" activity created a warm embrace and quiet "hum" of will-imbued security in which the children could harmoniously find their place in work and play.

In this book, Sarah has made a valuable contribution to the continued development of Waldorf parent/child work, so important in today's world. We can all be grateful to her.

Nancy Foster
WECAN Membership Coordinator

Preface

Many, many families meet Waldorf education for the very first time through the experience of coming together in a parent/child group—parents with their young children meeting other families in the context of the warmth and community to be found in a Waldorf school. And many young Waldorf schools, or groups hoping some day to become Waldorf schools, initiate this developmental path through the creation of just such a group. Parents with very young children yearn to find companionship with others who share their interests and values, and who seek a conscious relationship to the journey of being and becoming parents.

And so a remarkable diversity of opportunities for parents have been crafted to bring the nurturing of Waldorf early childhood education to families not quite within their homes, but within the home-like environment that a Waldorf early childhood teacher creates for those in her care. Here, many elements may weave together to enrich the lives of young families: a peaceful, beautiful and welcoming haven from the cares of everyday family life with young children; the delights of children sharing spontaneous, creative play both indoors and out; artistic activity for both parent and child; a shared meal; an opportunity to ask questions of the teacher-guide-facilitator who can share out of her experience and study.

These times together also provide vital support for parents in strengthening their individual approaches to living as a family, inspired by the sharing with other parents, the observations of children happily engaged in a child-friendly environment, and the many other aspects that the parent/child group may bring.

Those who are inspired to create such experiences for parents are seeking guidance and pictures of what others have done. Just as in a healthy nursery or kindergarten, the rhythm and content of the work is built up out of the particular circumstances in a given place. At the same time, the foundation principles of Waldorf education and anthroposophy offer the starting point.

Sarah Baldwin has wisely used her years in guiding the development of the parent/child programs at the Ashwood Waldorf School in Maine as the substance of this text. Conversations with Sarah over these years have given me a clear picture of the love and inspiration with which she carried this work. I am therefore delighted that she has put pen to paper to share her work with others, for it is often through the biography of another that we find a spark that illuminates our own paths. This book will offer much to those interested in this rich and rewarding work—accompanying families in the early years of their journeys. As Sarah tells us, although over 90% of Waldorf schools offer such programs, virtually nothing has been written about this important work. May her journey inspire others to share as well!

Susan Weber
Executive Director, Sophia's Hearth Family Center, Keene, NH

Introduction

*T*his book was inspired by what I had learned while teaching parent/child classes at Ashwood Waldorf School in Rockport, Maine, for three years. I began teaching parent/child classes in the fall of 1999, immediately after completing my Waldorf early childhood training at Sunbridge College. While parent/child work was mentioned occasionally and briefly during my training, nothing had really prepared me for the unique aspects of working with parents and children in this new and growing trend within Waldorf early childhood education. Even though it is estimated that over 90% of Waldorf schools presently offer parent/child classes[1], I discovered, much to my dismay, that few written resources (a few articles and no books) existed for the parent/child teacher.

I thus began by diving in headfirst, piecing together what I had learned from my training; from my experiences attending two different parent/child classes with one of my children; from attending workshops; and from mentors. Much of what I learned was gained through trial-and-error and observation. During my first year at Ashwood, I was determined to document what I had learned and what worked for me, for use by teachers, schools or individuals wishing to create a similar program—to give them a framework, at least, from which to start. My goal with this book is to help fill the void that currently exists

in written material for parent/child teachers. It is my hope that much more will be written about this important work within Waldorf education in the years to come.

I offer here one model of a parent/child program—the model that I used—but I have also included alternate ideas gleaned from colleagues teaching similar programs. My model may be considered as one possible way to set up a class for parents and children. One thing I cannot emphasize strongly enough is that *there is not one way or one "Waldorf-correct" model of offering such a class for parents and toddlers.* I am continually awed and inspired by colleagues who are creating new and innovative ways of working with birth- to three-year-olds, and am frequently envisioning things I might add or do differently with such a class in the future. One thing I've loved most about this work has been the creative freedom it affords, while working within a framework of Rudolf Steiner's views on child development and with the inspiration of anthroposophy.

This book presumes a certain familiarity with Waldorf early childhood education and anthroposophy. It is not intended as a guide for someone seeking to start such a program without having done at least some initial research into the methods of Waldorf early childhood education. Excellent books for someone seeking such introductory information are *You Are Your Child's First Teacher*,[2] by Rahima Baldwin Dancy, and *Beyond the Rainbow Bridge*,[3] by Barbara Patterson, a Waldorf parent/child teacher. Rather, this is intended as a practical guide peppered with personal insights, designed to inspire individuals to explore new ways of working with young children and their families. You will find very few "Thou Shalts" or "Thou Shalt Nots" in this book.

Finally, one last note of explanation: while the "parents" who attended my parent/child program were usually mothers, other caregivers—such as fathers, grandparents or nannies—were equally welcome. Whenever I refer to the "parent" in the "Parent/Child class," the parent participant referred to could just as easily be any of those adults.

Why Offer a Parent/Child Class?

I will never forget my first visit to a Waldorf kindergarten. I brought my then four-year-old son to the Pasadena Waldorf School for a kindergarten interview. I remember being enchanted by the beautiful, home-like room. I was impressed by the emphasis on the seasons, gardening and nature; the sense of reverence that was almost palpable in the room; the natural materials everywhere; and the smell of freshly baked bread. I remember feeling deeply moved by the archetypal images present in the room: the print of Raphael's "Sistine Madonna" and the crèche figures set up in anticipation of Advent. I remember the sense of knowing in my heart that this was absolutely the right environment for the young child. My heart quickened with excitement. Then I remember feeling absolutely crestfallen when I remembered that it was my son who would get to come here everyday, not me. It dawned on me then that I needed to be in this environment as much as my son did—if not more!

Since the birth of my first child, I had been considering a career change. I had long felt drawn to teaching, and had gone so far as to request catalogs from various teachers' colleges. I hadn't found many of the program descriptions terribly inspiring. I wasn't sure what or who or where I wanted to teach. But it was during that initial visit to the Pasadena Waldorf School that I had an "a-ha" moment. "This," I thought, "is where I was meant to teach!" I realized that if I were to become a Waldorf kindergarten teacher, I could come here everyday, too! At that moment, I asked the teacher, Amy Allesandri, about teacher training options. I enrolled in part-time foundation studies at the Waldorf Institute of Southern California within three months—before my son was even ready to start kindergarten!

Years later, after my experience first as a parent in parent/child programs at two different Waldorf schools (with my younger son), and having taught parent/child classes myself for three years, I am now aware that my initial experience at the Pasadena school was far from unique. Many parents are looking for exactly the same thing, often without realizing it. Some parents have a similar experience to mine—instantly recognizing something true as soon as they set foot in a Waldorf kindergarten classroom. For others, it is a vague feeling that deepens over time. Soon after I began teaching parent/child classes at Ashwood, I overheard a statement quietly made by one of the new moms to another mom after attending her first class, "I can see now that I need to bring more of this into my home life."

In these times of frantic schedules, non-stop activities, being bombarded by conflicting information from so-called "experts," and being faced daily with endless choices, parents—striving to provide the "best" for their children—are frequently left feeling dazed and confused. There is usually not enough quiet time in their lives to allow them to relax and breathe and listen to their intuition. A Waldorf parent/child class can offer parents this rare and precious gift. One of the mothers in my program told me that our Friday class was the highlight of her week—the thing she looked forward to most. It was the one time during the week when she felt herself relax, and she admitted that she probably needed the class more than her child did. We can provide quiet time, accompanied by simple activity—time for mothers and children to simply be with one another; opportunities for mothers to listen to their hearts.

Socialization and Community Building

*K*im Billington, a Steiner playgroup leader and Waldorf teacher in Australia, describes the purpose of a Waldorf parent/child class in her lecture, Creating a Steiner Playgroup: "The aim of Steiner playgroups is to develop a sanctuary of safe play for children and an oasis of peace and friendship for the parents."[4] I think this succinct description touches on an important aspect of parent/child classes.

I am a firm believer in the adage: "It takes a village to raise a child." I feel strongly that mothers were never meant to raise children, isolated, in nuclear families. I remember the loneliness of being a first-time mother, transitioning abruptly from being a creative career woman in a big city to suddenly finding myself home alone all day with a newborn infant. What might have developed into post-partum depression was almost instantly alleviated when I joined a playgroup of five or six mothers in my neighborhood with infants of the same age. The need for support, caring and friendship for new mothers cannot be overestimated.

I think that many parents are drawn to a Waldorf school because of the strong emphasis on community. Today's isolated parents are seeking that "village" of like-minded individuals with shared values in which to raise their children. While many parents are initially drawn to a Waldorf parent/child program because they believe their child needs an opportunity to socialize, more often than not, it is the parents who are in greater need of socializing!

Recognizing this, I felt it necessary to find a balance in class between quiet, purposeful activity while also allowing for quiet conversation. I did not discourage conversation among parents, but sometimes found it necessary to remind them to turn down the volume, or to not get so engrossed in conversation that they became unaware of their children.

Likewise, I also encouraged parents to socialize outside of class. Some of the parents in my classes would get together weekly at one another's homes, or meet for outings with their children. Other times, parents would take turns caring for each others' children to give mom or dad a break. It was always gratifying for me to see this happen because I find the value of community for both parents and children to be immeasurable. I tried to emphasize to parents at every opportunity that the social ties they formed while their children were young would prove invaluable as they continued their parenting and schooling journeys together in the years to come.

Care of the Senses

Another benefit of a parent/child class is offering parents and children an environment that is nourishing to the senses. It may be one reason that parents experience the feeling I had when I first set foot in a Waldorf kindergarten—a feeling of peace, contentment, and a sense of "knowing."

For children, care is taken to provide a classroom full of furnishings and playthings that are nourishing and pleasing to the senses: dolls made with cotton fabric and stuffed with wool; natural wooden playthings; hemmed squares of colored (often plant-dyed) silks; baskets of shells, stones, and blocks made from tree branches. All these serve to feed the senses in a different way from the hard plastic toys common in most pre-school environments. The aesthetics of the room, too, are intended to create an environment that's home-like and beautiful—warm, inviting and secure. One is likely to find soft pink- or peach-colored lazured walls, silk curtains and wooden furniture in an Waldorf early childhood classroom, all of which help create this mood.

Often, the environment of an early childhood classroom is an introduction for parents to a new way of thinking about children's playthings. Through direct experience, they come to appreciate the different qualities presented to the senses between hard, plastic, mechanical toys, and the more natural, less-formed playthings found in a Waldorf classroom. After joining a parent/child class, parents are often inspired to make different choices when choosing toys for their children. Sometimes parents will want to make a major transition at home—cold turkey, so to speak. I've always encouraged such parents to make the switch gradually, reminding them that wooden toys (while being of high quality and a good investment) are expensive. Trying to replace a child's playthings all at once with wooden toys would be quite a considerable expense! Rather, I have advised them to consider slowly replacing the plastic and "junk" with quality toys made of natural materials. When something new comes in, something goes out or may conveniently "disappear."

Inclusion of Parents

*T*he presence of parents in the classroom is often not encouraged in a Waldorf kindergarten. This is usually done in an attempt to create a sacred, safe space for the young child, protected from the distraction of visits by strangers. Unfortunately, this can sometimes lead parents to experience an air of mystery, a feeling of being unwanted, shut-out, or in the worst cases, create feelings of suspicion and distrust. In spite of a teacher's explanation, parents may be left wondering, "What really goes on in there, and why am I not welcome?"

A parent/child program allows parents to experience first-hand a typical Waldorf early childhood morning. They are often nourished and enriched by the activities offered. Their fear of the unknown is allayed, and they are better able to understand the gesture of loving protection created by the Waldorf early childhood teacher. Thus when their child moves on to a nursery or kindergarten program, instead of uncertainty, the parent is able to trust the teacher and have faith in the program, having gained knowledge of what goes on and why. Through their parent/child experience, parents come to appreciate the efforts of the teacher in creating a protected environment for the children, instead of feeling shut out as a brand new parent might.

When these children arrive for their first day of nursery or kindergarten, the family knows what to expect. They have been educated about the philosophy of Waldorf early childhood education and, one would hope, Waldorf education throughout the grades. They likely will have already adopted certain practices at home, such as having established rhythms, saying a blessing before meals, eliminating or limiting the child's media exposure, and so forth. This makes the work of the nursery or kindergarten teacher much easier, but most importantly, these changes will have been introduced earlier in the child's formative years to the great benefit of the child and his family.

Building Enrollment

*O*ffering a parent/child program can be one of the best tools for building enrollment in a Waldorf school. It can be seen as a year-long (or more) introduction and orientation to Waldorf education and to the life of a school.

I have found that it is important to find ways to make families in the parent/child program feel included in the life of the school. Not only is this of benefit to the new families, but it is also of benefit to the entire school. Parents of the youngest children are often still at-home parents with time and energy to devote to a school's fundraising and festival efforts. It also helps to forge what, we hope, will become a long-term relationship. Effective ways that I have found to include parents in the life of the school are by sending them the weekly school newsletter and inviting them to participate in school events, festivals, lectures and workshops. Inviting them to such events as "A Walk Through the Grades" or school assemblies is a wonderful way for parents of toddlers to get a glimpse of what lies ahead in the grade school.

As testimony to the effectiveness of a parent/child program as an enrollment tool, consider the following. By the end of the 1999-2000 school year, Ashwood Waldorf School had twenty-six children enrolled in the parent/child program. By the following September, all but four continued at Ashwood—either in the nursery or kindergarten (if they were old enough) or re-enrolled in the parent/child class. Of the four who left, two moved out-of-state.

And over the next few years, after committing to and expanding the parent/child program, Ashwood's early childhood programs grew from two under-enrolled kindergartens and a nursery in 1999, to three fully-enrolled kindergartens, a nursery and four parent/child classes four years later. As a result of the growing early childhood numbers, the first grade classes have begun to grow as the first parent/child graduates are entering the grade school. This has been a valuable enrollment tool in our small-town and largely rural area.

To Inspire and Improve the Quality of Family Life

*T*hrough our example and modeling, parents may be inspired to make changes in their lives at home. I feel it is extremely important not to verbally *suggest*, or worse, to lecture parents about making changes. It is easy for parents to feel inadequate when they compare themselves to a Waldorf early childhood teacher, or their homes to a Waldorf early childhood classroom.

Rather, through the parent's *experience* in the program and by the teacher's *example*, parents may see what is lacking in their busy, often chaotic home lives, and be inspired to make changes at home. Again, when *asked*, I advise parents to begin making changes in baby steps. One might start by simply lighting a candle and saying a blessing at dinnertime. Let each small change become a habit before introducing another one. Though one might be tempted to do a massive overhaul on family rhythms and routines, this is more likely to lead to frustration and confusion for the entire family. A parent evening discussion on "Rhythm at Home" can provide much inspiration and an opportunity for parents to share ideas.

What are the Qualities Required in a Parent/Child Teacher?

Comfort with Parents

*I*t goes without saying that a successful parent/child teacher should be comfortable interacting with both children and adults. This came naturally to me as a parent of young children myself, and as an extrovert. I couldn't imagine, at first, why this work wouldn't be easy for everyone. In time, I came to understand that not all my colleagues were as drawn to this work as I. Many early childhood teachers have chosen their profession because of their love of children, but are, in fact, less comfortable teaching with adults present.

I had one colleague who at one time felt she could never teach a parent/child class because she was not a parent herself. She felt that being a parent was a prerequisite, but I strongly disagree. Being a parent can certainly benefit a parent/child teacher, especially

in terms of having empathy for the challenges the parents of young children face, but it is certainly not a prerequisite. This colleague went on to teach a parent/child class, bringing many years of Waldorf experience, quiet wisdom, gentle humor and enormous artistry to her class. Our styles are decidedly different, but I believe both are suitable. I am grateful for the sake of the families in her parent/child class that she overcame her preconception of what a parent/child teacher should be.

In addition to a comfort-level with adult relationships, it goes without saying that a parent/child teacher must also be comfortable singing and "performing" in front of adults. I know early childhood teachers who love doing circle and puppet plays with their nursery and kindergarten classes, but who are nearly paralyzed with fear and self-consciousness when other adults are present. I think that for most of us, presenting a circle in front of adults for the first time can be intimidating, but I have found that it gets easier and easier the more often one does it.

Suspension of Judgment

This, I feel, is one of the most—if not *the* most important—quality essential for a Waldorf parent/child teacher. I have heard too many stories from Waldorf early childhood parents of how they felt judged by their child's teacher and were made to feel inadequate as a parent. They sensed (or worse, were *told*) that the teacher thought that their child was not dressed warmly enough; up too late the night before; not fed well enough; harmed by not having been breastfed; breastfed for too long; tainted by television; given the wrong kinds of playthings; (fill in the blank!). How can we expect to earn a parent's trust if we project these attitudes—even if they're unspoken?

One important lesson I learned from Susan Weber, Executive Director of Sophia's Hearth Family Center in Keene, New Hampshire, is that it is essential to accept parents who come to you *where they are, without judgment*. They are trying to be the best parents they can. I continually tried to cultivate a sense of gratitude for each and every parent who found their way to our program. In order to humble myself, I needed only to think back to my first two years as a parent, before I discovered Waldorf education, and to remember all the mistakes I made! Here is where being a parent can be helpful.

Again, I chose to offer assistance to parents through example; making books and hand-outs available; and offering advice only when asked, or when I sensed an appropriate "teaching moment." For example, two toddlers might be fighting over a toy; one parent might be trying desperately to reason with the children, initiating a discussion about "fairness" and "taking turns." I might then step in and invite one of the children over to the play kitchen to help me bake some muffins. Emily happily follows me to the play kitchen and the conflict is resolved. I have modeled for the parents how to use distraction to settle a conflict without any discussion.

A Feeling of Gratitude and Joy

One of the guiding principles of LifeWays, a professional development program and network for childcare providers, states that:

Children thrive in the presence of devoted caregivers who enjoy life and caring for children. This is the foundation for learning and healthy development. Young children learn primarily through imitation/empathy and, therefore, need to be cared for by people with integrity and warmth who are worthy of being imitated.[5]

Put quite simply, a teacher of young children should teach with joy and love.

This is a principle that I always strove for and came to quite naturally. I think it is one reason I had such a high retention rate, and why I continue to enjoy long-lasting and caring relationships with many of the families who came through my classes. A teacher's love for her work is palpable and brings joy to those around her.

I felt enormous gratitude for each of the children and parents who came to my classes—for the relationship we would share; for all that we had to teach one another; and for putting their faith in our program and in me as a teacher. As Rudolf Steiner reminds us, it is essential to our self-development to cultivate an interest in the other.

> ... [S]ympathy is awakened in the right manner if we take an interest in a being: and if, as anthroposophists, we set ourselves the task of extending our interests more and more, and of widening our mental horizon, this will promote the universal brotherhood of mankind. Progress is not gained by the mere preaching of universal love, but by the extensions of our interests further and further, so that we come to interest ourselves increasingly in souls with widely different characters, racial and national peculiarities, with widely different tempera-ments, and holding widely different religious and philosophical views, and approach them with understanding. Right interest, right understanding, calls forth from the soul the right moral action.[6]

I tried to learn as much as I could about each of the families in my classes—their life-style, background, profession, values, struggles, questions and so on. The interest that I tried to cultivate, and the genuine caring that resulted, added greatly, I think, to the depth of my relationships with the families in my classes, and aided the level of trust they were able to place in me.

Connection with Anthroposophy and Understanding of Waldorf Education

As with all Waldorf teachers, I believe that a Waldorf parent/child teacher ought to be, at the very least, familiar with and comfortable with anthroposophy. Ideally, this would come through teacher training, but might also come through extensive reading, study groups, workshops, conferences, and on-going study. I feel that one needn't necessarily be an anthroposophist, but that it is *essential* that the teacher be on a path of spiritual and personal development, and is striving to teach and act out of her highest self and out of the insights offered by anthroposophy.

Many questions are likely to come from parents in a parent/child program regarding anthroposophy—sometimes based on hearsay or misinformation. It is important for a parent/child teacher to be able to speak knowledgeably and with personal conviction about such matters.

Likewise, many questions will be asked about Waldorf education. Again, it is important for a parent/child teacher to have a solid understanding of the principles of Waldorf education and to be able to articulate them. Indeed, I consider it part of the parent/child teacher's job to educate and inform parents knowledgeably about Waldorf education and to be able to address their sometimes tough questions and concerns.

Waldorf Training

*B*ecause of the shortage of trained Waldorf early childhood teachers, many schools must rely on parents or untrained teachers to lead their parent/child classes. In many cases, talented individuals who are well-suited to this work, but without training, may be chosen to lead a parent/child class. A school might choose someone whose background includes, instead of training, extensive reading or study groups participation. It would be important for such a teacher (and important, too, for a trained teacher!) to seek out a mentor and to attend courses and conferences while serving as a parent/child teacher.

But I feel that *ideally* the parent/child teacher should have (or at least be enrolled in) Waldorf teacher training. Having a firm philosophical foundation and understanding of why one is doing what one is doing will only serve to strengthen the class. Without training, I would imagine it difficult for teachers to communicate with parents the whys and wherefores of what is being offered, or to answer parents' often demanding and probing questions about Waldorf education.

I am the first to admit that training alone does not necessarily a good teacher make, but if one has the other qualities mentioned previously, training can only strengthen the teacher, the school and the quality of the program offered. If a Waldorf school cannot find a trained, qualified teacher to lead its parent/child classes, I believe that the school should make every effort to help the untrained teacher receive the training. (Several WECAN-recognized training institutes across the country offer part-time early childhood trainings for teachers already employed in a Waldorf school—see **Appendix A**).

I've heard of many Waldorf schools that do not seem to regard their parent/child classes or teachers as important as their kindergarten or grade school counterparts. This, I feel, is a big mistake. Schools must recognize the importance of the parent/child program as the introduction many families will have to the school. A parent's first impression of the class and the teacher will greatly influence her future relationship with the school, and will probably determine whether or not that relationship is long-term. Spending the extra money to pay the salary of a trained teacher—or to train an untrained teacher—is, I feel, a wise and important investment for a Waldorf school.

Description Of My Parent/Child Program

Rhythm of the Year

*E*ach of my parent/child groups at Ashwood met for two hours once a week. During my first year, we offered three ten-week sessions. Currently, the school is offering two fifteen-week sessions (a fall session and a spring session). This decision was made because there was little turnover in the program. Most parents continued to enroll session after session, and offering two sessions, instead of three, cut down considerably on the administrative work of re-enrollment. A beginning parent/child program may choose to start by offering three sessions a year until one has a sense of how much continuity or turnover there will be.

I have heard of some Waldorf schools that have waiting lists for parent/child classes (time or space constraints may prevent a school from expanding the number of classes) and limit a family's enrollment to one session in order to allow new families to have an experience of the class. This, to my mind, is a big mistake. Many young families are drawn to Waldorf schools for the sense of community and shared values. I believe that once an opening is made for a family, there needs to continue to be a place for them and that the gesture of turning them away at the end of ten (or eight or twelve) weeks is not in keeping with the spirit of Waldorf education. My preference would be to see a family placed on a waiting list, if necessary, but once there is an opening, allowing that family to feel welcomed into the community as a full-fledged member for as long as they desire.

Rhythm of the Morning

*P*arents and children would arrive at 9:15 in the morning and the class ended at 11:15. Determining the right time for class to begin proved to be a bit tricky. For those parents who had older children in the school, it meant waiting forty-five minutes after dropping off their older children at 8:30. However, 8:30, or even 9:00 seemed to be too early for a lot of new moms with first-born toddlers to get up, get dressed, and get out of the house. After some shifting of class hours back and forth, and polling of parents, 9:15-11:15 is what seemed to work best for us.

At the end of class at 11:15, parents and children were invited to play outside in the early childhood play yard for as long as they liked. Most would stay outside until noon when the nursery and kindergarten mornings ended.

The rhythm of our morning was as follows:

9:15	Arrival: coats hung, slippers put on
9:15-10:00	Free play/Snack preparation/Craft activity
10:00	Clean up time/Set table for snack
10:15	Circle time/Handwashing
10:30	Snack/Dishwashing
11:00	Story
11:15	Outside play

Set-up

I would arrive at the classroom forty-five minutes ahead of time to prepare. Preparation for me meant making sure everything was tidy and in its place—making sure the room was beautiful, warm and inviting. I always had fresh flowers or a plant for the table. I then put out ingredients and supplies needed for the day's snack on one of two tables, and set out materials for our craft project on the other table. The oven was preheated if we were baking that day. The woodstove in my room would be lit with a fire if it was a cold morning.

Arrival

One of the most effective things I implemented was to inform parents ahead of time—before their first class—of what to expect. Each parent, upon enrolling, would receive a lengthy letter from me describing the program (see Appendix D). In the letter, I described the calm and quiet mood we were trying to create. I asked the parents to enter the room quietly and for both parent and child to bring a pair of slippers or warm socks to put on upon arrival. I found that making the expectations clear ahead of time went a long way to help create the right mood from the very beginning of the first class.

Crafts

I found it was important to remind parents, both in my initial parent letter and again at our first orientation meeting, that their attention must first be on their child, and secondly on the craft project. Parents should never feel like they must finish their craft project if their child obviously needs their attention. The craft projects were made available so that those parents whose children were playing happily in the room on their own could be engaged in and modeling real, meaningful work. Some parents would take their handwork and sit on the floor in the play area while their young children played; some would sit at the table doing their handwork while conversing quietly with the other parents; and others realized that their children were just too young or needing of their attention, and so either skipped the craft project or took it home with them to complete later.

Most of the craft projects I offered were simple enough to complete in one class, though occasionally we did more complicated projects, such as making knot dolls, that took several classes to complete. Another option is to have an ongoing project, such as knitting, that can be picked up and left off as needed. This also relieves the teacher of having to plan and prepare a different craft activity each week, and parents needn't feel rushed to finish a project before the class has ended.

Another project idea is to make things for the class. For example, during my first year teaching parent/child classes, I had the parents make little, child-sized aprons out of tea towels and finger-knitted cords to keep and use in the classroom. Similarly, one could have parents hem napkins and placemats for use in the class.

(**Appendix A** contains a list of sources for ideas for appropriate craft projects.)

Free Play

The first forty-five to sixty minutes of our class was an opportunity for free play. While snack preparation and a craft activities were offered at the two tables, the children were free to explore the room, either with a parent or on their own.

My room was equipped with a basket of "tree blocks"—unfinished, sanded sections of tree branches; a basket of colorful silks; four playstands with play clips; an assortment of dolls; a doll carriage; a doll cradle; a doll highchair; a basket of shells; a basket of bean-bags and felted balls; a small wagon for pulling; and a collection of stick horses (made

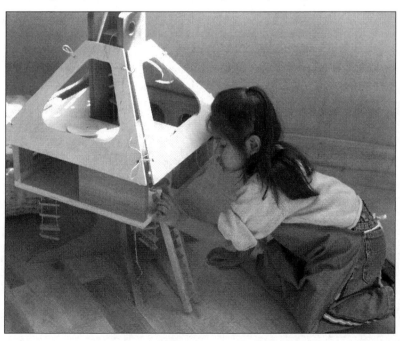

from broom handles with stuffed wool socks for heads). These are items typically found in a Waldorf kindergarten classroom. Other items I found nice to have for toddlers were a wooden rocking horse, wooden push toys, pull toys and stacking toys.

In addition to the afore-mentioned list, two of the most indispensable items in my classroom were the play kitchen (see **Re-sources**) and an antique, child-sized cradle. The play kitchen was in a corner of the room. Its boundaries were defined by two playstands hung with curtains. Within this area was a small, toddler-sized table with four chairs; a set of wooden play dishes set upon the table; a wooden play stove; a wooden play ironing board and iron; a small laundry basket; an assortment of child-sized aprons; and small shelves with play cooking pots and pans. This was perhaps the most heavily used area of the room. There were some children who seemed to spend the entire year in the play kitchen!

Having a real, child-sized cradle in the room was recommended to me by Louise de Forest, a former kindergarten teacher at Green Meadow Waldorf School in Spring Valley, New York. Not only did the toddlers in the program enjoy climbing in it and being rocked by mommies (or pretend mommies), but it was also useful to lay sleeping infant siblings in during program hours.

Some children needed mommy or daddy always by their side, while other children—often the older ones or those who had been in the program for a while—were content to play by themselves or with the other children while mother sat at the table, working on a craft project or helping with snack.

Domestic Arts

During the free play hour, there were always domestic chores set up and waiting to be done—washing placemats and napkins in two large galvanized washtubs with a washboard; hanging them to dry on a wooden drying rack; ironing placemats and napkins; and polishing our table or cutting boards. In my welcome letter to parents, I described the benefits to the children of being surrounded by loving adults engaged in meaningful work and asked each parent to try to engage in some of these housekeeping activities each week. Even though these were activities that many parents in the group never performed at home (many children in my class had never before seen an ironing board!), parents in the class usually seemed eager to help and enjoyed the calming effects of engaging in the domestic arts.

In my first year teaching the program, I set up domestic chores only occasionally as an activity offered in place of a craft. However, at the suggestion of Connie White, a pioneer parent/child teacher from London, Ontario, I began setting up domestic activities weekly at each class and found that it greatly added to the sense of calm purpose and meaningful work. This addition almost palpably helped to a weave a mantle of warmth and protection around the children in our presence. I highly recommend offering domestic activities as a regular part of one's program.

Clean-up and Table Setting

At the end of our free play hour, I would signal the transition to clean-up time by singing one of the following songs:

Let's put all our toys away
We will play another day

or:

Many hands make light work
Many hands make light work
Friends together, work together
Many hands

Parents and children would then begin helping to put away the toys and craft materials and to neaten and tidy our room. Once the room was tidy I would sing:

Polly put the kettle on
Polly put the kettle on
Polly put the kettle on
We'll all have tea!

This would let parents and children know that it was now time to set the table for snack. Chairs would be counted and placed around two long tables set end to end. Each place would be set with a small cloth napkin, a small porcelain cup, and a spoon (if necessary) for that day's snack. Two teapots full of warm herbal tea—usually peppermint, perhaps with elderflower or chamomile added—would be set at each end of the table. A candle, a snuffer, and box of matches were set in front of my place. The prepared snack food, I quickly discovered, needed to remain high on counters—out-of-reach from little hands—until we were actually ready to sit down for snack after circle time. Once the room was tidy and the table set, it was time for "Circle."

Circle Time

The transition to circle time was announced by singing "Let Us Form a Ring" from Nancy Foster's invaluable collection of the same title.[7] Upon hearing the song, parents and toddlers would gather together on the big braided rug in the center of the room, and take one another's hands to "form a ring."

I began every circle every time with the same sequence of verses and songs:

Sung:

Let us form a Ring
Dancing as we sing,
Ring-a-ring-a rei-a,
Ring-a-ring-a-rei-a,
All sit down upon the ground,
Watch the birds fly up and down,
Kick-er-I Kick-er-I kee![8]

Spoken, standing with gestures:

Down is the Earth, up is the sky
Here are my friends and here am I

Sung, seated on the rug:

Good morning, dear Earth
Good morning, dear Sun
Good morning, dear resting stones
And beasts on the run
Good morning, dear flowers
And birds in the tree
Good morning to you
Good morning to me

Spoken, seated, with simple gestures:

"Eee," said the bee, flying up in the tree
"Ah," said the stars, shining from afar
"Oh," said the gnome, all cozy at home

These would be followed by two or three simple finger plays, touching games (Wilma Ellersiek's books[9] are wonderful sources for these) or nursery rhymes, while remaining seated on the floor.

Originally, this was the extent of my circle when I began teaching the program. In the beginning, I modeled my circle on what I had seen other teachers do in parent/child classes and did not offer the kind of story/circle that is commonly offered in a Waldorf kindergarten. Then during my first year at Ashwood, Nancy Foster published her second anthology, *Dancing as We Sing*,[10] as a companion to *Let Us Form a Ring*. In this second volume, she included circles adapted for nursery classes. As I reviewed them, some of them seemed to me appropriate for a parent/child class, and so I experimented by offering the "Cat and Mouse" circle from this collection.[11]

I was pleased to discover that both the children and parents were responsive to this kind of circle that weaves verses and songs into a story theme, usually connected with the season. The children took great delight and participated more and more fully as we repeated the circles for many weeks. I also liked the fact that it gave the parents an experience of circle time as it is presented in the nursery and kindergarten. It was great fun to see parents crawling on hands and knees like a cat, trotting like a pony or hopping like a bunny. I think the parents enjoyed circle as much or more than their children did!

So the same sequence of opening songs and verses continued, followed by a seasonal theme circle. I continued to rely heavily on Nancy's nursery circles from *Dancing as We Sing*, as well as to create and adapt some of my own.

I was surprised by how many of the youngest children—even one-year-olds—participated vocally and with movement in the circles. But there were always some children—not necessarily the youngest—who resisted joining the circle, or who were not interested in participating. In my introductory letter I explained to parents that this is perfectly normal toddler behavior, and that parents should not feel stressed or worried if their child did not want to participate. In such cases, I requested that parents stay with their child in the room—rather than having the parent join the circle and leaving the toddler to his own devices—and suggested that the parent focus her attention on the circle from wherever she is in the room. I requested that the parent step out with the child only if the child was being disruptive to the circle—if, for instance, the child was having a tantrum.

On more occasions than I can count, parents have relayed to me stories of the child who seemingly never paid attention at circle time in class, who would then later sing every song and repeat every verse verbatim in the car, or at home at dinnertime. In these cases, I explained that even though a child may not appear to be participating outwardly, very often he is participating fully inwardly and taking everything in, unbeknownst to us.

Handwashing

Each circle time ended with the following song and served as a cue that it was now time to wash hands:

Wash hands, now
Our friends have gone to plow
It is time to wash your hands
Wash your hands now

Parents and children would then line up for the bathroom, where the sink had already been filled with warm soapy water. I used Dr. Bronner's lavender-scented soap for a warming and calming effect. One might wish to add some drops of lavender essential oil to the basin of water. Parents would help the children to wash their hands and to dry them with a towel. We always used terry bath towels, though some health departments insist on paper. When one mother once questioned me about the hygiene of sharing a cloth towel, I explained to her that children could use an antibacterial soap and paper towels, but as soon as they touched the door handle or held hands at the snack table, their little hands would be instantly covered again with germs. Using cloth towels is also gentler on the environment. Sometimes when we had a larger class, we would set up a second basin of soapy water on a small table to help hand washing proceed more quickly. After hands were washed, everyone took a seat at the snack table.

Snack

Once we were all seated at the table, I lit the candle in front of my place setting as we said the following verse together:

Fire spirit, fire sprite
Share with us your golden light
Come for us our candlelight!

Then parents and children would take hands round the table as we sang:

Earth who gave to us this food
Sun who made it ripe and good
Dearest Earth and Dearest Sun
We'll not forget what you have done.

(spoken):

Blessings on the meal and enjoy your snack!

Baskets of bread or fruit would then be passed round the table, or I would ladle bowls of rice, oatmeal or soup from my place and pass them. Herbal tea and water were the beverages offered at each class.

Typical Waldorf kindergarten snacks were served in my program: homemade bread, apples, oatmeal, brown rice, carrots, cornbread, freshly baked cookies sweetened with honey, homemade applesauce, vegetable soup, and so forth. My desire was to give parents some new ideas for healthy snacks that could be prepared at home; to show them that activities such as baking fresh bread and churning butter are wonderful experiences for young children and need not be intimidating or time-consuming; and to give them a taste, literally, of the kinds of snacks that are served in a Waldorf kindergarten. During the first half of the first year of the program, we prepared a different snack every week. However, after a conversation with Jill Bieber, former parent/child teacher at Green

Meadow Waldorf School in Spring Valley, New York, I reconsidered and decided to serve snacks in a three-week rhythm instead.

I found this new approach to be much more satisfying. The value of repetition for the children was immediately apparent. Not only did I observe the increasing ability of the children as they assisted with now familiar activities such as cutting vegetables or grinding grain, but I also observed their growing confidence in trying and enjoying the sometimes unfamiliar snack foods. Often a child would be too timid to try an unfamiliar food the first week; she might then have a nibble or two the second week; and then empty her bowl by the third week!

(Recipes for some of the snacks served in my program can be found in **Appendix C**.)

Dishwashing

When snack time drew to a close, I would ask a child to snuff our candle. Parents and children would help to clear the table and set up for dishwashing. During cleanup and table setting time, my assistant would fill two dishpans—one with soapy water and the other with clear rinse water. These dishpans would be brought to the table after snack, along with the compost bucket, wooden drying rack and some dishtowels. Some of the children would don aprons, roll up their sleeves (some mothers would simply undress their children, knowing how wet they would get!) and proceed to help wash the dishes. At this point, I would leave my assistant to supervise the dishwashing and cleanup while I began to set up for our story.

Stories/Puppet Plays

The stories I found most successful for ages one to three were very simple, short stories. Nature stories, animal stories and nursery rhymes all work well for this age group. While most of the Grimm's fairytales would not yet be appropriate for such little ones, I always told the story "Sweet Porridge"—perhaps the sweetest and simplest tale from Grimm's—at the end of the year, especially for the benefit of those children who were about to "graduate" to the nursery program.

I learned from Connie White and Rena Osmer that children under three benefit from having stories told with puppets or props since their capacities for inner picturing have not yet developed, so I always told my stories this way, though usually the set-ups were quite simple. The stories were always told from memory, "by heart"—never read.

It can be a challenge for a new teacher without a collection of puppets to come up with a repertoire of puppet plays, but I discovered that puppets can be made quite quickly and simply. With the advent of the miraculous "felting needle" (see **Resources**), puppets can be made very quickly with only some colored wool and the needle. A brightly colored silk scarf with just a knot for a head can become a giant or a troll. Of course, if one is working in a school with early childhood colleagues, one could always borrow puppets from other teachers.

Sometimes I would set up the story on a small, low table, and other times I would set it up on the floor. Next to the story set-up would be a stump covered with a silk or two, a small vase of flowers, a "story candle" and snuffer. When I sang in the mood of the fifth, "Storytime at the Ashwood Tree"—the traditional call to storytime in all the Ashwood early childhood classes—parents and children would know it was time to come over to

the big, braided rug, and toddlers would hop happily into a big person's lap.

Once everyone was seated, I would light the story candle and sing:

Here is a spark
of Father Sun's light
See how it keeps us
so warm and bright.

If the story was a fairy tale, I would sing "Mother of the Fairy Tale."[12] For other stories,

I would sing a song tied to its theme as an introduction. The stories told were short—usually no more than five minutes—in an effort to hold the attention span of the youngest members of our group. As with circle time, I explained to parents that some toddlers are just not able to sit still for even a five-minute story. Again, I did not insist that all the children sit quietly for the story, but requested that if a child was being noisy or disruptive during the story, that the parent take her out for this brief period of time. By and large, there were few problems, and I was always pleasantly surprised at how the stories captured and held the attention of even the very wee ones.

I usually told three different stories over the course of the ten-week session. I usually told one story for the first three weeks; a second story for the next three weeks; and a third for four weeks. Frankly, I believe that one could easily get by with telling only two stories over ten weeks—five weeks each—and that the children would benefit from the repetition and familiarity. The children never seemed to tire of hearing the same story week after week. I think I felt compelled to change the story more often hoping not to bore the parents!

Nursery rhymes are the simplest stories and are entirely appropriate stories for this age. Other stories that I used and found worked well were:

"The Three Little Kittens"

"The Giant and the Gnome"[13]

"The Little House"

"Stone Soup"

"Sweet Porridge"[14]

"The Turnip"

"The Little Red Hen"[15]

"The Mouse Who Wanted His Tail Back"[16]

"Brown Bear, Brown Bear What Do You See?"[17]

"The Three Billy Goats Gruff"[18]

(The stories above that are not cited in the endnotes are included in **Appendix B.**)

One of the first mistakes I made in teaching parent/child classes happened when I told "The Three Billy Goats Gruff" as the first story at my first class, at the suggestion of a mentor. I had been taught in Waldorf early childhood teacher training to tell stories as they are written and not to tamper with the language, which is often ripe with symbolic meaning, rich language and meaningful archetypal images. And so I memorized "The Three Billy Goats Gruff" as it was written, verbatim, translated from the Norwegian. At the climax of the story, the big billy goat says:

Well, come along! I've got two spears,
And I'll poke your eyeballs out at your ears;
I've got besides two great, flat stones,
And I'll crush you to bits, body and bones.[19]

In the afternoon, after I had told this story for the first time, I had a concerned parent call me at home to tell me how uncomfortable it made her. She was worried that her two-year-old daughter would now be inspired to poke other children in the eyes. I tried to explain to her about the rich language of fairytales, their symbolism and the archetypes they represent. I tried to reassure her that hearing the story was unlikely to turn her daughter into a violent eye-poking monster. Yet I hung up feeling that we really had not heard each other and wondering if I was ready to take on this work.

I reflected on the conversation for quite a while, and then referred to Rahima Baldwin Dancy's list, adapted from Joan Almon's "Choosing Fairytales for Different Ages," in *You Are Your Child's First Teacher.*[20] I was surprised to discover that "The Three Billy Goats Gruff" was a story recommended for four- to young five-year-olds! I wondered how my mentor could have led me astray. I felt I had no choice but to call this poor mother back, and acknowledge that I had made a mistake. The next week I told a different story.

A few weeks later I attended a workshop with Connie White for Waldorf parent/child teachers. In describing her program, Connie mentioned telling the story of "The Three Billy Goats Gruff." Needless to say, as soon as I could, I cornered her to question her and shared my story. "Well," she replied, "of course I don't leave in the part about poking the eyeballs out at the ears!" It was then that I learned that minor adaptations to good stories to suit the needs of one- to three-year-olds are not a crime.

In the spring, I brought "The Three Billy Goats Gruff" back, but this time with a slightly altered ending:

I've got two great spears, and two flat stones,
I'll crush you to bits, body and bones!

The children were delighted by the story, and I never heard another word of concern. I continued to tell the story every year and it was always a favorite.

Another wonderful idea for storytime in a parent/child class comes from Suzanne Down, founder of Juniper Tree School of Story and Puppetry Arts in Boulder, Colorado. Suzanne has created a "story apron" covered with many decorative pockets in which hide small felted finger puppets. Her apron is a whimsical creation with ribbons, feathers and bells adorning it. She will invite a child to choose a pocket, then with great reverence and ceremony, take the puppet carefully from her pocket and place it lovingly on her finger, sometimes with a silk draped over her hand before placing the puppet on her finger. For each puppet, she has prepared a little verse or nursery rhyme, and has carefully choreographed precise gestures and movements that magically bring each puppet to life. One could choose three or four children each time to choose a pocket at storytime.

Suzanne has a series of seasonal collections of poems and stories, as well as puppet-making kits that are wonderful resources for parent/child teachers and highly recommended (see **Appendix A**).

Connie White used a similar story apron to tell the story "Brown Bear, Brown Bear, What Do You See?," adapted from the Eric Carle picture book of the same name, which I also used in my program (see **Appendix B**). In this story, all the animals are hidden in pockets of the story apron and come out one by one as each is discovered by the preceding animal.

Goodbye

At the end of our story, I would snuff the candle. In my early classes, I made the mistake of asking a child to snuff the candle, which seemed to work well at snack time. For some reason, however, it seemed to turn into a competition at storytime, with several children all lunging for the candle at once. So, instead, "Miss Sarah" always snuffed at the end of each story. We then recited the following verse together:

May the light of love live in my heart,

Merry meet and merry part and merry meet again.

Then sang the following song:

Goodbye now, goodbye now

We leave you now and home we go

Goodbye now, goodbye now

Goodbye to all of you!

This concluded our formal morning together, and at this point parents and children were invited to play outside in the early childhood play yard.

Outdoor Play

After story, parents and children would gather their things and bundle up to play outside. Originally, they were invited to join Ashwood's nursery and kindergarten students on the playground, but this became problematic. I loved the idea of these parents being able to observe our early childhood students on the playground. I remember how impressed I was by observing the children's play on one of my early visits to a Waldorf school.

As our parent/child classes grew, it became apparent that the sheer number of people on the playground was becoming a problem. The nursery and kindergarten teachers had a difficult time keeping an eye on their charges, with all the extra active toddlers in their midst. Additionally, there were a few instances of parents taking charge and speaking to the nursery and kindergarten students in ways deemed inappropriate by the early childhood teachers; their methods of settling disputes, while well-intended, were not always the same methods the teachers used.

We resolved this problem by creating a special play area for the parent/child children just outside the back door of our classroom, around the corner from the kindergarten playground. A lovely sandbox was created out of a natural embankment of large stones, which lent a protected feeling—like a little hideout. We also hung a couple of toddler swings from the trunk of a tree that had been cut and affixed horizontally between two standing trees. A grove of pine trees stood just beyond.

This special play area worked quite well. Their play was visible to me, and if someone needed the bathroom, they could easily come in through the back door. The mothers seemed to enjoy socializing together afterwards and often enjoyed picnics with the children during warmer weather. They were free to play outside for as long as they liked. There were also areas of the grade school campus that were accessible to them, such as a large wooden ark that was a favorite place to eat lunch.

I am aware that some parent/child programs include time for outdoor play in the middle of the morning. At the parent/child group I attended with my son at Highland Hall Waldorf School in Northridge, California, outdoor play was scheduled after snack and before story. While the children played outside, the teacher set up her story. I have also heard of programs that conclude the morning with a walk—parents, children and teacher together. My former assistant, who is now teaching parent/child classes, is doing this. I think a nature walk together, watching the seasonal changes over the course of the year, is a lovely idea.

Should a Parent/Child Teacher Have an Assistant?

*T*his is not an easy question. When I was hired at Ashwood, it was presumed I would need an assistant. However, the teachers of the two different parent/child classes I had attended—which, at that time were my only frame of reference—worked without an assistant. "Why," I asked myself, "would I need an assistant when I will have eight-ten pairs of adult hands available to help each day?" I convinced my colleagues at Ashwood that I didn't need an assistant and urged them to save their money.

So, during my first year I worked alone and relied on the parents in the class to help. I was able to carry it off, but I found that parents weren't always the eager helpers I had hoped. Often they were engaged in their handwork project, with their child, or in conversation with one another. Sometimes, I felt resentful that they didn't seem conscious of all that needed to be done, and learned that I wasn't good at asking for the help I needed. Often I felt like my back was to the group, busy at the counter or stove with snack preparation or cleanup, and unaware of what was going on in the room. When I attended the workshop with Connie White, she appeared incredulous that I could work without an assistant!

After the first year, my colleagues and I reassessed the situation, and it was decided that we would ask a parent in the class to assist in exchange for free tuition for the program. Having someone delegated whom I could ask for help was better, but still not ideal. At this point, I was teaching four different classes, four mornings a week, and I had two different assistants. One was herself a kindergarten teacher and was intuitive about what needed to be done and was a tremendous help. Her child had graduated to kindergarten, and so she didn't have a child in the class. She was eager to learn Waldorf methods to incorporate into the public kindergarten where she taught.

The other mother who assisted me had a child who was needy of her attention. Not only was this mother often distracted by her child, but she sometimes seemed to be more interested in socializing with the other parents rather than attending to the needs of the class. I came to realize that every parent in the class needed to make her child her primary focus. I felt that it was not keeping in the spirit of what we were offering to ask a mother to divide her attention in this way.

Before beginning my third year, I rather sheepishly went back to my colleagues and asked if I might still have that assistant who was offered at the outset, and whom I so confidently rejected initially. Fortunately, it was agreed to, and my wonderful assistant, Toki Oshima was hired. Having someone paid to assist—however paltry the salary—made all the difference. I no longer felt like I was imposing by asking someone to do things. We developed a wonderful working relationship, and she was able to substitute when I was sick. She attended foundation studies in anthroposophy while assisting me, and through her experience working with me, Toki was able to take on the parent/child program as lead teacher when I, out of necessity, took a nursery/kindergarten class.

So, to answer the question, my feeling is that one does not necessarily need an assistant to teach a parent/child class, but if a school or program's budget allows, a paid assistant is wonderful to have!

Parent Education

*P*arent education can take many forms within the context of a parent/child class. What follows are a number of ways in which I tried to educate parents in my program.

Conversations During Class

While I tried to keep conversation quiet and minimal during the course of our morning, snack time, I discovered, was a wonderful opportunity to discuss parenting issues. It is perhaps the most social part of the morning, and the time lends itself well to conversation. A mother might raise a question, for instance, about lack of sleep. Usually I would let other parents share their advice and stories before voicing my own opinion. My style has always been not to offer my opinion too readily without being asked, but often at the snack table many eyes would turn toward me for a suggestion, and I found that many prime "teaching moments" presented themselves at the snack table.

One must be careful, of course, to always be mindful of the presence of the room. On occasion, I found it necessary to ask a parent not to talk specifically about her child in the child's presence, or not to discuss inappropriate news events—but this was rarely a problem. The parents in my classes most often impressed me with their tact and sensitivity.

I know of several parent/child teachers who have tried to incorporate formal parent education within the course of their morning program. For some, this has meant having the children go outside with an assistant, while the teacher led a discussion with parents on various parenting themes. My initial reaction to this idea was skeptical, and my intuition was reaffirmed by the opinion of Connie White. Connie's feeling is that parent/child programs should celebrate the togetherness of parents and children, and that separating parents from their children was not in the spirit of what we are trying to offer. I had to agree, and further suspected that it would be difficult for mothers to participate fully if their child was experiencing separation- or stranger-anxiety. How could a mother be expected to concentrate on the discussion if she could hear her child crying outside, or in the next room, as one- to three-year-olds are so naturally inclined to do? Therefore, I decided to offer parent education in the evenings instead, accepting that full attendance could not be expected.

Parent Evenings

About a week before the first class of each year, I offered a special orientation evening for parents who were new to the program. This was an opportunity, beyond the parent letter, to let parents know exactly what to expect, and to give them a picture of the mood we were trying to create before attending their first class with their child. The most successful orientation evening I had was based on an idea given to me by Rena Osmer, now Director of Early Childhood Teacher Training at Rudolf Steiner College in Fair Oaks, California.

Before parents arrived, I had set up various areas in the room for domestic activities: the ironing board, iron, and a basket of cloth napkins needing ironing were set up; two washtubs and a washboard and a drying rack were readied for washing dirty napkins and placemats; polishing wax and cloths were laid out on the table. After introductions were made and a brief overview of the program was given, I explained to the parents that we would spend the remainder of the meeting engaging ourselves in the domestic arts. I asked them to divide themselves into three groups and asked each group to go to one of the three "work stations"—ironing, washing or polishing. Then I explained that we would do our work with *no talking*; however, they were free to sing or hum as they worked. I told them that after a period of time, I would ring a bell and they were to proceed to the next activity. This would be repeated once more so that every participant would have time at each of the three domestic activities set up.

I will never forget the magic that was created the first time we did this. Everyone dutifully began his or her work as asked, albeit with a good deal of self-consciousness. I began humming a tune, wondering if anyone would join in. Shortly thereafter, one of the dads in our group, who was a sailor, started singing a sea shanty—a tune familiar to many of our group who reside in coastal Maine. It was not quite what I had imagined, but soon we were all singing along to these traditional work songs, happily engaged in our work. Those who didn't know the songs quickly learned the choruses and joined in.

After a time, the sea shanties died out and it got quiet again. The self-consciousness, however, had disappeared. Everyone now seemed deeply engaged with the tasks-at-hand. Then someone started softly singing "White Coral Bells." More voices soon joined in, and we had a lilting three-part round going as we completed our work. It was an unforgettable experience that brought tears to my eyes.

Afterward, we gathered together again to discuss what the experience was like. I think the key to a successful parent evening is to offer parents such an experience and then have them share with each other their personal experience of it, rather than have the teacher as "expert" lecture to the group on the finer points of parenting. It not only helps to build community within the group, but it is also a much more powerful learning experience. The parents who had attended the orientation evening, came to the first class the following week with a deep understanding of the mood and intent of the class—far deeper than could ever be conveyed by a letter alone.

I continued to offer at least one parent evening during each of the three ten-week sessions, for a total of four parent evenings during the year. I tried to choose topics for discussion based on suggestions from the parents, or on what seemed to be living in the group. Some of the topics we covered were: "Creative Discipline," "Nutrition and Warmth," "Toys and Playthings," "Rhythm in the Home," and "Celebrating Festivals." I found Margaret Shean Ris's master's thesis on the topic of parent evenings for parent/child classes[21] to be inspirational and informative. Margaret used the festivals of the year as a framework for her parent evenings; each parent evening centered on a different seasonal festival. She suggests that each meeting have a thinking, feeling and willing component to it. After reading her thesis, I always tried to incorporate this threefold idea into each of my parent evenings.

The "thinking" aspect often came through an article or chapter we would read together and discuss on the topic at hand; "feeling" came through reflections and sharing of our own childhood experiences; and "willing" came through activities offered at each meeting, such as the domestic arts (as described above), or an artistic activity such as painting, eurythmy, beeswax modeling, and so on.

One problem with parent evenings can be attendance. It is difficult for parents of infants and toddlers to get out in the evenings. Of course, it is always ideal if both parents can come, but that can be complicated and expensive if it means hiring a babysitter. I scheduled parent evenings at the beginning of the year and put the dates on the class calendar that I distributed to parents at the beginning of each session. This way, they had plenty of notice in order to plan ahead. I would also offer frequent reminders in class in the weeks leading up to our parent evenings. I found that usually about half the families would attend. I was sympathetic to those who were unable to make it, and would distribute notes and handouts from our meeting at the following class. I would also try to initiate a discussion about the meeting at snack time for the benefit of those who were unable to attend.

Handouts

I tried to have a handout every week for parents. They were usually articles on such parenting subjects as child development, media, sleep, nutrition, toys, education, discipline, warmth, and so on. Many were from Waldorf sources, but my some of my favorites handouts were media articles based on current research that supported the wisdom of Waldorf education. These articles have become increasingly plentiful, and I never was at a loss for a handout to provide. Other times I would copy handouts passed on to me by other teachers, articles from Renewal, or chapters from books, such as *You Are Your Child's First Teacher* or *Beyond the Rainbow Bridge*. Before a parent meeting, I would usually send home a handout to be read ahead of time and discussed at the meeting.

In addition to handouts on parenting topics, I tried to always provide a handout each time our circle changed with the words to all the songs and verses printed. I included musical notation when possible. Parents expressed much appreciation for this. Several, though, said they had trouble remembering the tunes and could not read music and asked for a tape of me singing them for their own use (not to be played for the child). I thought this was a good idea and hoped to try it, but never got to it. One might want to give it a try.

Nancy Foster shared with me her experience of originally giving the parents in her parent/child classes at Acorn Hill a copy of the words and music to her current circle. Later, when those parents' children were in kindergarten, they had come to expect handouts of the circle. The kindergarten teachers, however, were reluctant to do this since it allowed them less flexibility, and the parents were no longer present to experience how the circle was actually done. Therefore, one might wish to confer with the teachers ahead before providing copies of circle material. One could provide instead, as Nancy now does, handouts only for the "daily" songs and verses—those that are used at each class—for example, the welcome verse, meal blessing, goodbye song, and so forth.

Lending Library

I always kept a lending library of my own personal books on child development, parenting, Waldorf education and anthroposophy in the classroom for the use of the parents in my classes. I am happy to say that the books were heavily used and are now dog-eared. There is only so much that can be conveyed in class and through parent evenings. I was pleased that so many parents took an interest and wanted to know more about the ideas underlying Waldorf education.

In addition to the small lending library in my classroom, the school had a much larger lending library, open to the community, which I always made sure parents knew they were invited to use.

Phone Hours

In my letters to parents, I encouraged them to call me at home if they ever had any questions or concerns. Some years I specified "calling hours," which were the times when I was most free to talk. This policy was never abused, but rather created the opportunity for dialogue. I always tried to express my appreciation of parents' willingness to share their concerns. I think it contributed to the open, caring and trusting relationships I established with many of the parents in my classes.

Study Groups

Occasionally, Ashwood would offer study groups on parenting issues during the morning with infants and toddlers welcome. These were usually offered by the school administrator and would focus on a book or series of lectures. These were wonderful opportunities for deepening one's understanding of Waldorf education, and I always made sure the parents in my classes knew about them, and encouraged them to attend.

Communication

I believe it is important to help parents enrolled in a parent/child program feel like full-fledged members of the school community. It is easy for them to feel like outsiders looking in. Welcoming them to take part in the full life of the school is more likely to make them feel like part of the community and to result in student retention. Keeping parents informed was accomplished in a number of ways:

Letters

In addition to the initial letter all parents in my program would receive, I also tried to send at least one additional letter per session to review parent evenings, to remind them of upcoming events or to comment on the program.

Newsletter

As soon as a new family enrolled, I made sure their name was added to the school's weekly newsletter mailing list so that they would be informed of school-wide events, as well as to get a glimpse into the life of the school.

Bulletin Board

In addition to the various bulletin boards around the school, we had our own bulletin board just outside the classroom door. Here I would post reminders about upcoming events at Ashwood, community events, or articles of interest.

Class Roster

At the beginning of each session, I would provide each family with a roster of the names, addresses and phone numbers of all the participants in the class. They would receive this along with a calendar for the session noting any holidays or vacation weeks. Providing a roster, I feel, is important for fostering community and friendships among the parents in a class.

Publicizing the Program

We were fortunate at Ashwood to have a dedicated and energetic admissions director, who, together with her husband, a talented graphic designer, produced an eye-catching and attractive flier for the program.

Beginning in August of my first year, these fliers were placed in prominent places throughout the community. Excellent places to publicize are midwives' offices, obstetrician's offices, pediatrician's offices, libraries, community centers, and homeopathic or naturopathic doctor's offices. Press releases with a photo were sent to local newspapers. At the beginning of each new session, we would repeat these efforts.

I was hired to teach one parent/child class per week, or two if enrollment was sufficient. Not only did we have two full classes by the beginning of September, but we also added a third class by the second session. By September of the following year, we were offering four mornings a week of parent/child classes—no small feat for a small-town school in a rural community!

Another idea for publicizing such a program is to offer a free class at a local library, making sure to have enrollment forms on hand at the end of the class. We also made sure to have parent/child information on-hand whenever there has been a public performance of a puppet play by our early childhood teachers.

Once things were off the ground, the best publicity was word-of-mouth. Word quickly got around about the unique program our school was offering, and many parents had friends enroll over the ensuing months. It got to a point where all our classes were full and we had to stop advertising!

Space Considerations

I was fortunate and grateful to have my own classroom (though I did share my room with the Aftercare program). The year I came, Ashwood had just completed building Rosewood, its new early childhood center. The building is beautiful, with wood floors with radiant heat; each classroom has its own kitchen, bathroom and woodstove.

I have talked with other parent/child teachers who were not so lucky and had to put up with less-than-ideal circumstances. I was sympathetic when I learned that Connie White, a veteran Waldorf early childhood teacher, had to teach in a church room in which she had to move all the furniture and toys out at the beginning of each class, only to pack them all up and put them away again at the end. No wonder she needed an assistant!

Unfortunately, it seems that many Waldorf schools do not yet view their parent/child programs as being as important as the kindergarten and grade school classes. Parent/child classes are often relegated to using a kindergarten classroom in the afternoons (not prime-time for toddlers!), if not off-campus in a rented church basement or similar venue. I think this is a big mistake.

For the reasons stated previously, I feel it's important for parent/child classes to be on campus in order for parents to feel like members of the community and not second-class citizens. If a school's goal is to build enrollment through the parent/child program, then it is extremely valuable for those parents to become familiar with and see the other teachers, children, buildings and classrooms.

Unfortunately, however, space is at a premium in most schools and is simply not available. Ashwood is now, in fact, facing this same dilemma. When Rosewood was being built five years ago, the Board of Trustees in 1999 feared that building a third classroom was excessive and would never be filled. It was decided then that the third classroom could be used at least one day a week for a parent/child class and in the afternoons for the aftercare program. By September 2004, early childhood enrollment had grown so rapidly that all three classrooms in Rosewood were occupied five mornings a week, but unfortunately, the school had to cut back on the number of days that parent/child classes could be offered.

One solution proposed for the future would be to build, or move to, a small home-like cottage near Rosewood in which to house parent/child classes, the aftercare program and perhaps a new parent/infant program. This would have the advantage of being on the main campus, yet would provide a protected, home-like environment for Ashwood's youngest students.

Furnishing the Space

What are the minimum requirements for furnishing a parent/child classroom? To offer a program such as mine, one would need to at least have a large table or two—child-height—and enough child-sized chairs to seat everyone. Although child-sized chairs are not terribly comfortable for adults, this seemed to work fine and no one ever complained. (There were always a couple of rocking chairs available for visiting grandmothers, or someone with back problems.)

Access to a bathroom is, of course, essential. It is nice, if possible, to have a changing table

in the bathroom. I tried to keep an extra supply of diapers and wipes for mothers who occasionally caught themselves empty-handed.

If one is planning to prepare and serve snack as part of the program, then one naturally needs a means to cook. I was fortunate to have a kitchen in my classroom, but one could also make do—as I've seen other teachers do—with a plug-in electric burner or two for heating water for tea and preparing snacks, such as oatmeal or soup; and a large size electric oven—larger than a toaster-oven, smaller than a range—for baking. Ideally, one would have a sink in the room, but it is possible to get by with a couple of dishpans for washing dishes.

One would also need a supply of cooking pots, pans and utensils; enough child-sized bowls and cups—I preferred ceramic ones—to accommodate everyone; a teapot and tea-kettle for heating water; dishpans; dish rack—I preferred a wooden one; dish towels; and potholders. Two of the favorite items in my kitchen were not essential, but wonderful to have: a wooden grain mill and a glass butter churn (see **Resources**). Grain grinding and butter churning were favorite activities on bread-baking days. One would also probably want to have a candlestick or holder, a supply of beeswax candles and a candle snuffer for snack and storytime.

A rug is nice, if not essential, for circle time. I had a large, braided wool rug that lent a homey feel to the room. A few playstands can go a long way to create separate play areas in a large, open room. As I described earlier, I found setting up a corner of the room as a "play kitchen" to be invaluable. Within this area I recommend having a small, child-sized table and chairs; a play stove; wooden dishes; play pots and pans; aprons; a play ironing board and iron; utensils; and so on. Doll cradles and dolls can live in this area as well. (See **Resources** for sources for many of these items.)

For laundry activities I had two large, galvanized wash tubs, a couple of small, child-sized washboards, a collapsible wooden laundry drying rack, a supply of clothespins, a clothes-line outside, an ironing board and iron. I would always set up the wooden play ironing board and iron next to the adult-sized one so that parent and child could iron together. Often, mother would hand a warm, freshly-pressed napkin to her toddler who would give it a finishing touch with his wooden iron!

Additional playthings one might wish to have were described earlier in the section on "Free Play."

What Ages?

When I first arrived at Ashwood, the program had already been advertised and promoted for children from eighteen months to three years. I was comfortable with this, but nervous when some fifteen- and sixteen-month-olds seemed to have slipped through the cracks and registered for the program. Before the first class began, I spoke to the parents of the younger children and tried to explain that their child might be too young to get much out of the program. I was met, however, with parents who seemed absolutely hungry to join the program—my sense being more for themselves than for their children—and so I agreed to try it.

What I discovered was that not only were the younger children not a problem, but that they were also easier participants than some of the older and more active children. The mothers of those youngest children of that first year went on to become some of the most dedicated parents in the school; their children are still enrolled and they are active school community members.

During my second year, we had a request from a mother of a one-year-old to join the parent/child program. Again, I was reluctant, but this mother had already been in a parent/child class for one- and two-year-olds with Andrea Gambardella at the Baltimore Waldorf School. This mother appeared to be committed to Waldorf education and was anxious to continue her involvement within a Waldorf community. How could I say no?

I again experienced no problems having a one-year-old present, and so we changed the ages of our program to include one- to three-year-olds. Through my experience with this range of ages, I have become committed to the idea of mixed ages together. My opinion in this matter has also been influenced by the ideas of Helle Heckmann as described in her book, *Nøkken: A Garden for Children.*[22] Helle offers a Waldorf-based childcare program in Denmark for children from one to seven years old. She states in her book:

We also find it is important for the whole group to be together: even the "difficult" six-year-olds will demonstrate their sense of care when they look into the eyes of a one-year-old and see the need for a helping hand. The young children learn to play through observing the older children. [Emphasis mine.] Being left alone to look at other children playing is the best way to learn. … The mixed-age group benefits all the children, because the greater the age range, the easier it is to find a perfect match, and this spans all age groups.[23]

I found the benefits of mixed ages together to be no less true in a parent/child setting than in a childcare program such as Helle's. Having mixed ages together more closely mimics the natural dynamics of family life. As Helle points out, younger children learn to play by observing older children. And older children need to learn to be gentle and nurturing when younger children and babies are about (one reason that babes-in-arms were always welcome in my classes).

I have heard of Waldorf parent/child classes that are segregated by age—for instance a class for one- to two-year-olds, and another for two- to three-year-olds, but I consciously chose not to work this way and found the results satisfying. I always warned the parents of under-two-year-olds that circle time and storytime were apt to be the most challenging parts of the morning for their children. I explained that their child might find it hard to sit still for these more structured parts of the morning, and that that was developmentally to be expected. I invited parents to attend quietly to their child in these circumstances, or to step outside with their child for these brief parts of the morning, if necessary. With this understanding, we rarely had a problem and enjoyed the company of these youngest children and their parents. I believe it was these parents who reaped the greatest benefits from the program—receiving information and a new model of parenting when their children were still quite young.

Who's in Charge?

*E*arly on during my first year of teaching parent/child classes, I discovered that it is important to clarify this question with parents. Before I had a clear policy, I found that parents often didn't know what to do when their child was displaying behavioral problems in class. There might, for instance, be a temper tantrum resulting from a sharing incident. Often in these cases, I would find parents looking at me imploringly, wondering what they should do.

I came to understand that I was more teacher of the parents than of the children. The children were in the company of their trusted parent, and the parent is the primary authority figure in the child's life—not me, the "teacher" (whatever that can mean to a two-year-old!) whom they see for only two hours, once a week. Therefore, I felt it best for parents to try to resolve conflicts with their children first. In my initial letter to parents (see **Appendix D**), I assured them that I would step in to help if necessary, but gently reminded them that they were responsible for their own children during class and needed to be attentive to them at all times. I found that making this expectation clear at the outset went a long way to alleviate such situations of confusion about who's in charge.

I feel it is important to likewise remind parents that attentiveness to their child is paramount, and that they should not get so involved in socializing with other parents that they become unaware of their child's actions. They needn't be by their child's side the whole morning—in fact, it is best if they are not. As Helle Heckmann states:

An adult should never play like a child. The adult should be around, engaged in adult activities and not be a playmate. The adult may initiate play, but must at all times be conscious of his or her role and know when to leave the children to play on their own terms. Children should not depend on adults to participate in their games nor on adult attitudes. Free play will come from the children's own imagination, inspired by adults' working, songs, and stories, as well as everyday events.[24]

Ideally, parents can be sitting at the table working on crafts, or engaged in domestic activities, but like a teacher, they need to develop the "eyes in the back of their head" to always be aware of their child and his activity in the room.

Field Trips

When I began my parent/child classes, I had never heard of parent/child teachers offering field trips, but nevertheless was inspired to do so. I thought it would be a wonderful opportunity for parents in the different groups to meet each other, as well as a way to build and strengthen relationships among our enrolled families. I tried to offer at least one field trip per session. Our field trips were usually held on a day when no parent/child classes were scheduled and were open to all parent/child families regardless of what day they attended. Some of the field trips I offered were:

* Apple picking at an organic orchard. The apples were then used at snack time in the ensuing weeks (homemade applesauce became one of our snacks). This gave the children a nice connection with our snack time food and a sense of where our food comes from.

* A trip to a small dairy farm where the children were able to help milk a cow, to make (and eat!) fresh mozzarella cheese and to pet the variety of animals who lived there: Jersey cows, calves, pigs, sheep, pygmy goats, chickens and ducks.

* A visit to a local sheep farm to see baby lambs in the spring.

* A picnic at the beach in early June.

Festivals

*I*n addition to inviting parent/child families to all our school-wide festivals, such as the Michaelmas Festival and the May Festival, each year I invited my parent/child families to

share a Harvest Festival with our off-site kindergarten in Lincolnville, Maine. Spindlewood, as the kindergarten in Lincolnville is called, is a special place. It was the original home of the Ashwood school—an enchanted cottage in the woods on the property of Susan Silverio, the kindergarten teacher at Spindlewood and Ashwood's founding teacher.

During this festival, we gathered together outside under the apple trees together with Susan's class in late September. We shared the Harvest circle we had been working on since the beginning of the year, then Susan's class shared their similar circle with us. Together we proceeded to actually thresh and flail wheat while singing. After our work was done, we gathered for a snack of freshly-baked harvest bread and apples. This was followed by a craft activity such as braiding the wheat stalks to make crowns, and then the morning ended inside with a story.

While I always informed and invited parents to our school-wide festivals, I found the opportunity to share a festival with one or two other classes to be a special opportunity to deepen the parents' understanding of festival life in a Waldorf school, without being as overwhelming as the school-wide festivals.

Birthdays

I was unprepared for how I would celebrate birthdays in the parent/child program when the first birthday approached during my first session teaching. A day or two before the birthday, I found myself emailing colleagues for advice. I received a few suggestions, but the most helpful reply came from Connie White, who shared with me what she did.

She reminded me that two- and three-year-olds are usually still self-conscious and not ready to be singled out for special attention by a teacher. They also usually lack the attention span for the traditional kindergarten birthday story. Connie told me that she only celebrates birthdays in her parent/child program if the child's *actual* birthday falls on a class meeting day. Birthdays are still a novel and abstract idea for toddlers, and having a class celebration on a day other than their actual birthday probably only adds to their confusion. Connie would recognize the birthday child briefly during the beginning of her circle time by saying something like:

On this very day, three years ago,

Chloe came down from heaven and was born into the arms of love.

And today she is three-years-old!

I took up Connie's suggestion and chose to recognize birthdays this way. As short and simple as the above verse is, its simple but truthful image often left many of the mothers misty-eyed. I also offered to let the birthday child wear a gold birthday cape and gold paper crown during the circle—though usually only the older and more outgoing children would accept the offer. The gold crown was their gift to take home and was always eagerly received.

In addition to the recognition the birthday child received at circle time, we would also make "birthday muffins" for our snack that day (see **Appendix C** for recipe). I would put one rainbow candle on the birthday child's muffin, and we would all sing "Happy Birthday" at snack time. The candle, like the crown, would go home with the child. This simple celebration seemed to be just enough for this age, and the parents always seemed proud and appreciative of the recognition of their child's special day.

Question of Continuity of Care

One of the biggest and most compelling issues that arose for me during my years teaching parent/child classes at Ashwood was the question of continuity of care for the young child. The question initially arose for me at the beginning of my second year at Ashwood. I was in my room setting up for our class when one little girl, who had been with me for a full year in the parent/child class during the previous year, peeked in. She had such a look of confusion on her face. She looked at me as if to say, "I thought this was my room and you were my teacher," yet her mother was pulling the now three-year-old from my room and trying to push her next door toward the nursery classroom.

Throughout the year, I got similar looks from the children I had taught the year before when I saw them on the playground. At three, they were not yet very verbal, but their faces, to me, said it all. I began to question the experience of a very young child going from one teacher one year in parent/child to a second teacher the next year in nursery, and finally to a third teacher for a year or two in the kindergarten. So many changes before the child had even reached first grade! What sense did it make, I wondered, for a Waldorf school to strive to provide a child with one teacher from first through eighth grade, and yet give the very youngest children the experience of three (or more) different teachers before the age of seven?

The need of young children for consistent caregivers is well-researched and well-documented. In fact, the opening chapter of *The Irreducible Needs of Children*, by T. Berry Brazelton, M.D. and Stanley Greenspan, M.D., is titled "The Need for Ongoing Nurturing Relationships." In this chapter, the renowned pediatrician and the leading researcher on children's brain development begin their book by stating:

Although consistent nurturing relationships with one or a few caregivers are taken for granted by most of us as a necessity for babies and young children, often we do not put this commonly held belief into practice. The importance of such care has been demonstrated for some time. [25]

Similarly, LifeWays North America (see following section—**Other Programs**) lists as one of its principles for caring for young children:

Having consistent caregivers (over several years) is essential for young children, especially from birth to three years old and, preferably, up to primary school age.[26]

I have spent the ensuing months and years pondering the question of how to achieve continuity of care for young children in Waldorf early childhood programs.

Let us look for a moment at the evolution of early childhood programs within the Waldorf school movement. The first kindergarten class at the original Waldorf School in Stuttgart did not come into being until after Rudolf Steiner's death in 1925. For decades, the only offering for children under seven in a Waldorf school was the traditional Waldorf mixed-age kindergarten for four- to six-year-olds. In more recent years, nursery programs were added as it became the cultural norm for three-year-olds to attend pre-school. Most Waldorf schools responded to this need by offering a separate nursery program for three- to four-year-olds. The first parent/child classes began to be offered by some pioneering schools only within the last twenty years (though the majority of programs seem to have been developed within the last decade). This usually meant adding another separate class that children could enroll in before nursery or kindergarten. Today, as some schools are adding parent/infant classes to their offerings, it could mean up to four separate programs offered, sometimes with as many different teachers, before the child reaches first grade.

How can we remedy this situation? I have consulted with colleagues such as Susan Howard, Rena Osmer, and Cynthia Aldinger on this question. After considerable thought, I have come up with three alternatives that Waldorf schools could adopt to ensure more continuity of care for their youngest students.

1) As the LifeWays principle suggests, it would be ideal if children could have one teacher from birth to primary school age. Could Waldorf early childhood teachers adopt a model not unlike that of a Waldorf class teacher? In this scenario, a teacher could start working with a parent/child or parent/infant group, working with the family and offering parent education. As the group matures, the teacher could continue with the same group of children, now without the parents, through the nursery and kindergarten years until the children are ready for first grade.

Imagine how well that group of parents, children and the teacher would get to know each other. Imagine the level of trust that could be built up over a period of several years. Imagine the growth that a teacher could experience in stretching herself, perhaps out of her comfort zone, in working with children from as early as birth to age six—much as a class teacher stretches herself from first to eighth grade.

Helle Heckmann has achieved such continuity of care in her program, Nøkken, though she has achieved this through having one- to six-year-olds together in one program. The many benefits of having mixed ages together are well-documented in her book of the same title.[27]

2) Of course, the ideal is not always practical or realistic. Perhaps a teacher's greatest strength is in working with parents, or in meeting the needs of six-year-olds. Rena Osmer suggested that the next best thing would be to limit a child's experience to two teachers before first grade—one from birth to three, and the other from four to six. This could mean having one teacher offering parent/infant and parent/child classes for birth to three-year-olds, and then have the children "graduate" to a mixed-age kindergarten for, perhaps, three-and-a-half to six-year-olds. The child would then stay with the second teacher until he is ready for first grade.

3) A third scenario could preserve the nursery program. Some schools, parents and teachers have expressed the desire to protect younger three-year-olds from older and more active six-year-olds. In this case, it might be possible to have one teacher teach parent/child classes (and perhaps a parent/infant class) two days a week, and teach a nursery

program for three-year-olds the other three mornings. Then at age four, the child would move on to the traditional kindergarten for four- to six-year-olds. This scenario thus ensures continuity for the birth to three-year-old, and limits the number of teachers before first grade to two.

Other Programs for Birth to Three-Year-Olds

New models of working in a Waldorf-inspired way with children from birth to three are developing and blossoming throughout the U.S. at a rapid pace. Below are just a few examples of Waldorf early childhood programs that have found innovative ways of working with parents, infants and young children. I offer a glimpse at some alternatives to emphasize again that there is no one model for working with parents and that this is work that is growing and evolving.

Acorns and Oaks

Barbarina Heyerdahl, formerly of the Acadia Waldorf School in Bar Harbor, Maine, created a unique program for expectant parents, parents of newborns, infants and grandparents called "Acorns and Oaks." Barbarina recognized the value of providing expectant parents—some of whom might never have held or diapered a newborn—an opportunity to connect with mothers of infants. She also recognized the need of grandmotherly women in the community (not necessarily biological grandparents of the infants in the class) to be around babies and to share their wisdom. "Grandmothers" and teen mothers are invited to attend the program free of charge. New mothers may receive a welcome break, having their baby held for a while by an expectant mother or grandmother.

Barbarina was also inspired by the work of French obstetrician, Michel Odent, author of *Birth Reborn*[28], who recommended singing as beneficial breath-work for the expectant mother in preparation for childbirth. Recognizing the benefit of singing for the expectant mother, new mother and babies, one-half hour of each Acorns and Oaks class is devoted to singing together. The rest of class time is spent on weekly check-ins with each parent; discussions on different parenting themes such as sleep, immunizations, and so forth; and sharing a simple snack together.

FamilyWays and PlayDates

Rena Osmer, Peggy Alessandri and Lauren Hickman developed a program at Rudolf Steiner College in Fair Oaks, California called "FamilyWays and PlayDates" for parents, grand-parents, nannies, caregivers, and their young children (birth to age six). This program consists of two components: an evening discussion group for parents only, and a Saturday morning playgroup. Participants were able to register for one or both components.

In the evening discussion group, parents were invited to explore modern family issues through lively, educational conversations. In addition to discussions on child development, self-development and parenting styles, the group participants also celebrated festivals together, made toys and shared stories of family life. The activities of the Saturday morning "PlayDates" included finger plays, songs, crafts, stories, puppets, playtime, snack, walks, and child observation.

LifeWays North America

LifeWays was founded in 2001 by Cynthia Aldinger, a former Waldorf kindergarten teacher who served on the board of the Waldorf Early Childhood Association of North America for fourteen years. Cynthia helped to develop a ground-breaking program in East Troy, Wisconsin, that served as a new model for childcare for infants and young children.

One of the impulses that Cynthia Aldinger has brought to parent/child work through her work with LifeWays has been that of the "bodily care" of infants and children, and the "nurturing arts." In a parent/child class this could mean an emphasis on touching games between parent and child, and also bringing new consciousness to routine but nurturing acts such as diapering, hand-washing, tooth-brushing, hair-brushing, and so forth. It could also include rituals such as washing hands and face before snack time with warm washcloths scented with lavender oil, or foot baths followed by a massage with scented lotion

Today, LifeWays provides programs for caregivers, parents and parent educators and practical, hands-on programs for parents and grandparents to support and strengthen the growing child and family. Through LifeWays, a network of home and center-based

childcare providers throughout North America is providing quality childcare, adhering to "LifeWays Principles for Caring for Young Children" (see **Appendix F**). LifeWays offers part-time professional development programs for parents and childcare providers in several locations throughout North America.

Sophia's Hearth Family Center

Susan Weber, former Waldorf early childhood teacher training coordinator at Antioch New England Graduate School, serves as the executive director of Sophia's Hearth Family Center in Keene, New Hampshire. Founded in 1998, Sophia's Hearth offers classes for expectant and new parents; nutrition workshops; parent/child playgroups; infant massage classes; and speaker and discussion series. Sophia's Hearth programs are inspired by the insights of Rudolf Steiner, as well as Hungarian pediatrician Emmi Pikler and Magda Gerber, founder of RIE (Resources for Infant Educarers).

Parent-Led Playgroups and Parent Handwork Groups

Another option for parents seeking social connection with one another in a Waldorf setting is to meet as a more informal "playgroup." There might be an appointed parent "leader"— perhaps someone with more Waldorf experience than the others—or it might be more of a cooperative effort. Such groups might meet at someone's home; rotate meeting at different members' homes; or gather in a church or other community meeting place. This may be the best option for parents if there is no Waldorf school or formal parent/child group in their area.

Such a playgroup might include free play, handwork or craft activities; sharing snack; circle time; storytime; and outdoor play. Parents may choose to have a study group as well, reading and discussing books on parenting, Waldorf education or anthroposophy. One advantage to a parent-led playgroup that parents express is the freedom from judgment they feel by not having a teacher present (another important reason for teachers to guard against a tendency to pass judgment). Some parents are more comfortable among a group of peers, struggling together and supporting one another.

Other groups meet primarily to do handwork together with toddlers present. I was part of such a group at Green Meadow Waldorf School when my youngest was about two. We would meet to knit or sew toys and playthings while our older children were in school. We learned new skills from each other, created handwork projects to raise funds for the school, and enjoyed tea and conversation on a weekly basis.

Afterword

As I began writing this book, I did not think that I would find so much to say on the subject of parent/child work, and yet I feel I have only scratched the surface. It is my hope that other teachers can take some of the ideas presented here and create new and inspired approaches to working with young children and their families.

I also hope that through this effort more Waldorf schools will come to recognize the value and importance of parent/child classes. Margaret Ris summed up the benefits of a parent/child program to a Waldorf school in her thesis, *Festivals as Framework*:

Educating parents about Waldorf education before they enroll their children seems an optimal model in many ways. Parents will know more about what the school is about and, if they choose to continue with Waldorf education, they will be more involved and invested. Schools will enjoy a parent body that is knowledgeable and committed from the start. And children will have been raised more consciously. This foundation will allow them to fully thrive in a Waldorf setting later.[29]

But most importantly, it heartens me to think of the children and their families whose lives might be touched, or even changed, by the ideas I have laid out here—when new ways of parenting are discovered and families find support, community, beauty, joy and love in a Waldorf class for parents and children.

Endnotes

1   Margaret Shean Ris, *Festivals as Framework: A Model for Parent Education in a Waldorf School Parent-Tot Program*. 2001. Keene, NH: Antioch New England Graduate School Master's Thesis, p. 76.

2   Rahima Baldwin Dancy, 2000. *You Are Your Child's First Teacher*. Berkeley, CA: Celestial Arts.

3   Barbara Patterson, 2000. *Beyond the Rainbow Bridge*. Amesbury, MA: Michaelmas Press.

4   Kim Billington, 1991. *Creating a Steiner Playgroup: Guidelines for Working with Parents and Being with Very Young Children*, http://steiner-australia.org/other/playgroup.html.

5   From LifeWays North America's pamphlet, *LifeWays' Principles for Caring for Young Children*. (See **Appendix F**.)

6   Rudolf Steiner, 1996. *The Spiritual Foundation of Morality: Francis of Assisi & the Christ Impulse*. Hudson, NY: Anthroposophic Press.

7   Nancy Foster, 1989. *Let Us Form a Ring*. Silver Spring, MD: Acorn Hill Waldorf Kindergarten and Nursery.

8   C. Hodnett & K. Perlas in Foster, *Let Us Form a Ring*, p. 31.

9   Four books of Wilma Ellersiek's gesture games, verses and songs are available: *Giving Love-Bringing Joy: Hand Gesture Games and Lullabies in the Mood of the Fifth* (2003), *Gesture Games for Spring and Summer* (2005), *Gesture Games for Autumn and Winter* (2007), *Dancing Hand—Trotting Pony* (2010). All Spring Valley, NY: Waldorf Early Childhood Association of North America. A Spanish translation of selected games, *Juegos de Gestos de Mano*, is also available from WECAN.

10 Nancy Foster, 1999. *Dancing as We Sing*. Silver Spring, MD: Acorn Hill Waldorf Kindergarten and Nursery.

11 Foster, *Dancing as We Sing*, pp. 20-21.

12 Foster, *Let Us Form a Ring*, p. 31.

13 Bronja Zahlingen, 2005. *A Lifetime of Joy*. Spring Valley, NY: Waldorf Early Childhood Association of North America, p. 39.

14 The Brothers Grimm, with introduction by Padraic Colum, 1972. *The Complete Grimm's Fairy Tales*. New York: Pantheon Books, pp. 475-476.

15 Zahlingen, in Foster, *Let Us Form a Ring*, p. 58.

16 Learned from Susan Silverio, Waldorf early childhood teacher, Ashwood Waldorf School, Lincolnville, ME; attributed to Joan Almon.

17 Eric Carle, 1996. *Brown Bear, Brown Bear, What Do You See?* New York: Henry Holt & Co.

18 Joanna Cole, Editor, 1982. *Best-Loved Folktales of the World*. Garden City, NY: Doubleday & Co., pp. 326-327.

19 Cole, *Best-Loved Folktales of the World*, p. 327.

20 Baldwin Dancy, *You Are Your Child's First Teacher*, p. 207

21 Ris, *Festivals as Framework*.

22 Helle Heckmann, 1998. *Nøkken: A Garden for Children—A Danish Approach to Waldorf-Based Child Care*. Wilton, NH: Center for Anthroposophy.

23 Ibid., pp. 30-31.

24 Ibid., p. 31.

25 T. Berry Brazelton, M.D. and Stanley I. Greenspan, M.D., 2000. *The Irreducible Needs of Children*. Cambridge, MA: Perseus Publishing., p. 1.

26 *LifeWays Principles for Caring for Young Children*.

27 Heckmann. *Nøkken: A Garden for Children—A Danish Approach to Waldorf-Based Child Care*.

28 Michel Odent, 1994. *Birth Reborn*. Medford, NJ: Birth Works.

29 Ris, *Festivals as Framework*, p. 75.

Note:

Unattributed material has been learned or handed down from other teachers and colleagues in the oral tradition. If anyone knows the origin of the material, I would be grateful to learn the sources and give credit where credit is due. Please feel free to contact me at:

sarah@bellalunatoys.com

Sarah Baldwin—A Short Biography

Sarah Baldwin was born in Chicago and was raised as a bi-coastal child—growing up in both Los Angeles and New England. She studied theatre at Bard College and graduated from New York University with a degree in theatre. She worked as an actress in New York City for ten years.

Upon the birth of her first child in 1992, Sarah's life changed profoundly and irrevocably when she recognized that children were meant to be her life's work. She taught music-and-movement classes for parents and toddlers; began a support and activity group for stay-at-home-mothers; and worked in mainstream preschool settings in Los Angeles before enrolling in the part-time teacher education program at the Waldorf Institute of Southern California in 1996. She completed Waldorf early childhood teacher training in 1999 at Sunbridge College in Spring Valley, N.Y., and received an M.S.Ed. in Waldorf early childhood education in 2004.

Sarah taught parent/child, as well as nursery and kindergarten classes, at Ashwood Waldorf School in Rockport, Maine over a period of ten years.

The mother of two Waldorf graduates, Sarah is now the owner of Bella Luna Toys, an online source of Waldorf toys and art supplies, and writes about Waldorf education on her blog, "Moon Child": sarahbaldwin.com.

Bibliography

Almon, Joan, (Ed.) *An Overview of the Waldorf Kindergarten:* Articles from the Waldorf Kindergarten Newsletter 1981 to 1992, Silver Spring, MD: Waldorf Kindergarten Association of North America, 1993.

Almon, Joan, (Ed.) *A Deeper Understanding of the Waldorf Kindergarten:* Articles from the Waldorf Kindergarten Newsletter 1981 to 1992, Silver Spring, MD: Waldorf Kindergarten Association of North America, 1993.

Baldwin Dancy, Rahima. *You Are Your Child's First Teacher*, Berkeley, CA: CelestialArts, 2000.

Billington, Kim. "Creating a Steiner Playgroup" (transcript of lecture published on-line): http://steiner-australia.org/other/playgroup.html, 1991.

Brazelton, T. Berry, M.D. and Stanley I. Greenspan, M.D. *The Irreducible Needs of Children*, Cambridge, MA: Perseus Publishing, 2000.

Callan, Ginny. *Horn of the Moon Cookbook*, New York: Harper Perennial, 1987.

Davy, Gudrun and Bons Voors, (Eds.). *Lifeways: Working with Family Questions*, London: Rudolf Steiner Press, 1996.

Fenner, Pamela Johnson and Karen L. Rivers, *Waldorf Education: A Family Guide*, Amesbury, MA: Michaelmas Press.

Foster, Nancy. *Let Us Form a Ring: An Acorn Hill Anthology*, Silver Spring, MD: Acorn Hill Children's Center, 1989.

Foster, Nancy. *Dancing As We Sing: Seasonal Circle Plays & Traditional Singing Games*, Silver Spring, MD: Acorn Hill Children's Center, 1999.

Heckmann, Helle. *Nøkken: A Garden for Children—A Danish Approach to Waldorf-Based Childcare*, Wilton, NH: Center for Anthroposophy and Silver Spring, MD: Waldorf Early Childhood Association of North America, 1998.

Jaffke, Freya. *Work and Play in Early Childhood*, Hudson, NY: Anthroposophic Press, 1996.

Kenison, Katrina. *Mitten Strings for God: Reflections for Mothers in a Hurry*, New York: Warner Books, 2000.

König, Karl. *The First Three Years of the Child*, Edinburgh: Floris Books, 1998.

Mellon, Nancy. *Storytelling With Children*, Gloucestershire, UK: Hawthorn Press, 2000.

Patterson, Barbara and Pamela Bradley. *Beyond the Rainbow Bridge: Nurturing Our Children From Birth to Seven*, Amesbury, MA, 2000.

Ris, Margaret Shean. *Festivals as Framework: A Model for Parent Education in a Waldorf School Parent-Tot Program*, Keene, NH: Antioch New England Graduate School Master's Thesis, 2001.

Schmidt-Brabant, Manfred. *The Spiritual Tasks of the Homemaker*, London: Temple Lodge, 1998.

Smith, Patti and Signe Eklund Schaefer, (Eds.) *More Lifeways: Finding Support and Inspiration in Family Life*, Glouscetershire, UK: Hawthorn Press, 1997.

Steiner, Rudolf. *The Essentials of Education*, Hudson, NY: Anthroposophic Press, 1997.

Steiner, Rudolf. *The Spiritual Foundation of Morality: Francis of Assisi & the Christ Impulse*, Hudson, NY: Anthroposophic Press, 1996.

White, Connie. "Adult Activity in the Parents and Tots Program," The Waldorf Kindergarten Newsletter, Spring 1998, pp. 18-20.

Thomson, John, (Ed.) *Natural Childhood: The First Practical and Holistic Guide for Parents of the Developing Child*, New York: Fireside, 1995.

Appendix A

Resources

General Resources

Art and Craft Supplies

Bella Luna Toys
3 Gordon Dr., Rockland, ME 04841 / 888-438-1299
www.bellalunatoys.com
Carries a wide selection of art supplies and craft materials.

Halcyon Yarn
12 School St., Bath, ME 04530 / 1-800-341-0282
www.halcyonyarn.com
Carries a good variety of wool, yarn, felting needles and other handwork supplies.

Mercurius U.S.A.
c/o Gayle Griffiths, 7426 Sunset Ave., Ste. C, Fair Oaks, CA 95628 / 916-863-0411
Fax: 916-863-5309
www.mercurius-usa.com
Primary supplier of Waldorf school supplies in U.S. and Europe.
Sells only to schools and homeschool cooperatives.

Paper, Scissors, Stone
PO Box 428, Viroqua, WI 54665 / 888-644-5843
www.waldorfsupplies.com
Carries art and handwork supplies.

Books

(Good sources for many of the titles listed in the Bibliography and this Appendix.)

Waldorf Early Childhood Association of North America
285 Hungry Hollow Rd, Chestnut Ridge, NY 10977 / 845-352-1690
info@waldorfearlychildhood.org
store.waldorfearlychildhood.org

The AWSNA Bookstore
www.awsnabooks.org

Bob & Nancy's Bookshop
www.waldorfbooks.com

Rudolf Steiner College Bookstore
9200 Fair Oaks Blvd., Fair Oaks, CA 95628 / 916-961-8729
www.steinercollege.edu/store

Waldorf Toys

Bella Luna Toys
3 Gordon Dr., Rockland, ME 04841 / 888-438-1299
www.bellalunatoys.com
*Most of the Waldorf toys and playthings recommended in this book
can be ordered online from Bella Luna Toys.*

Teacher Education and Professional Development

Professional Organizations

Waldorf Early Childhood Association of North America
285 Hungry Hollow Rd, Chestnut Ridge, NY 10977 / 845-352-1690
info@waldorfearlychildhood.org
www.waldorfearlychildhood.org

Waldorf Early Childhood Teacher Education

The following training centers were members of WECAN at the time of printing. Please visit www.waldorfearlychildhood.org for a current list of member training centers.

Full Members

Bay Area Center for Waldorf Teacher Training, San Rafael, CA
  415.479.4400 / contactus@bacwtt.org / www.bacwtt.org
Rudolf Steiner College, Fair Oaks, CA
  916-961-8727 / rsc@steinercollege.edu / www.steinercollege.edu
Rudolf Steiner Centre Toronto, ON, Canada
  905-764-7570 / info@rsct.ca / www.rsct.ca
Sunbridge Institute, Chestnut Ridge, NY
  845-425-0055 / info@sunbridge.edu / www.sunbridge.edu
Waldorf Institute of Southern California, Northridge (LA) and San Diego, CA
  818-349-6272 / office@waldorfteaching.org / www.waldorfteaching.org

Developing Members

Alkion Center at Hawthorne Valley, Ghent, NY
  518-672-8008 / info@alkioncenter.org / www.alkioncenter.org
Great Lakes Waldorf Institute, Milwaukee, WI
  414-616-1832 / lori.barian@greatlakeswaldorf.org / www.greatlakeswaldorf.org
Sound Circle Center, WA
  206-925-9199 / information@soundcircle.org / www.soundcircle.org
Waldorf Institute of Southeastern Michigan, MI
  734-635-4143 / www.wism.org
Waldorf Teacher Education Eugene, OR
  541-686-9112 / office@wtee.org / www.wtee.org
West Coast Institute, Sechelt, BC, Canada
  604-740-0539 / info@westcoastinstitute.org / www.westcoastinstitute.org

Other Professional Development Opportunities

Juniper Tree School of Story and Puppetry Arts
720-438-8344 / suzanne@junipertreepuppets.com
www.junipertreepuppets.com

LifeWays North America
Central Office, c/o Cynthia Aldinger, Executive Director
403 Piney Oak Dr., Norman, OK 73072
405-579-0999 / CynthiaA@lifewaysnorthamerica.org
www.lifewaysnorthamerica.org

Sophia's Hearth Family Center
700 Court St., Keene, NH 03431 / 603-357-3755
info@sophiashearth.org
www.sophiashearth.org

Resources for Circle Time Material

Aulie, Jennifer and Margret Meyerkort (Eds.). *Spring; Summer; Autumn; Winter; Spindrift;* and *Gateways* (a series of six collections of poems, songs and stories for young children), Stourbridge, UK: Wynstones Press, 1999.

Darian, Shea. *Seven Times the Sun*, Philadelphia: Innisfree Press, 1994.

Down, Suzanne. *Around the World With Finger Puppet Animals: Resource Book #1*, Boulder, CO: 1999.

Down, Suzanne. *Autumn Tales: A Seasonal Collection of Poems and Stories for Early Childhood Teachers and Parents*, Boulder, CO: Storyarts Publications, 2000.

Down, Suzanne. *Spring Tales: A Seasonal Collection of Poems and Stories*, Boulder, CO: Story-arts Publications, 2000.

Ellersiek, Wilma. *Giving Love—Bringing Joy: Hand Gesture Games and Lullabies in the Mood of the Fifth*. Spring Valley, NY: Waldorf Early Childhood Association of North America, 2003. A learning CD is also available.

Ellersiek, Wilma. *Gesture Games for Spring and Summer.* Spring Valley, NY: Waldorf Early Childhood Association of North America, 2005. A learning CD is also available.

Ellersiek, Wilma. *Gesture Games for Autumn and Winter.* Spring Valley, NY: Waldorf Early Childhood Association of North America, 2007. A learning CD is also available.

Ellersiek, Wilma. *Dancing Hand—Trotting Pony.* Spring Valley, NY: Waldorf Early Childhood Association of North America, 2010.

Ellersiek, Wilma. *Juegos de Gesto de Mano.* Editorial El Liceo, Spain (available from WECAN).

Foster, Nancy. *Dancing As We Sing: Seasonal Circle Plays & Traditional Singing Games,* Silver Spring, MD: Acorn Hill Children's Center, 1999. A learning CD is also available.

Foster, Nancy. *Let Us Form a Ring: An Acorn Hill Anthology,* Silver Spring, MD: Acorn Hill Children's Center, 1989. A learning CD is also available.

Foster, Nancy (ed.). *The Seasonal Festivals in Early Childhood: Seeking the Universally Human,* Spring Valley, NY: Waldorf Early Childhood Association of North America, 2010.

Jones, Betty. *A Child's Seasonal Treasury,* Berkeley, CA: Tricycle Press, 1996.

Lebret, Elisabeth. *Pentatonic Songs: For Nursery, Kindergarten and Grades I and II,* Toronto: The Waldorf School Association of Ontario, 1985.

Lonsky, Karen. *A Day Full of Song: Work Songs from a Waldorf Kindergarten,* Spring Valley, NY: Waldorf Early Childhood Association of North America, 2009. A learning CD is also available.

Opie, Iona A. & Peter Opie (Eds.). *The Oxford Dictionary of Nursery Rhymes,* Oxford, UK: Oxford University Press, 1998.

Scott, Anne. *The Laughing Baby: Remembering Nursery Rhymes and Reasons,* New York: Bergin & Garvey Publishers, 1987.

Thienes-Schunemann, Mary. *Sing a Song of Seasons; The Singing Baby; This Is the Way We Wash-a-Day; The Wonder of Lullabies;* four volumes from the *Singing With Children Series,* E. Troy, WI: Naturally You Can Sing Productions, 2000-03.

Resources for Craft Projects Suitable for a Parent/Child Class

Armes, Jean Paccagnan. *Felted Treasures: How to Felt & Sculpt Wool with a Felt Needle*, West Vancouver: Heaven & Earth, 2002.

Berger, Petra. *Feltcraft: Making Dolls, Gifts and Toys*, Edinburgh: Floris Books, 1994.

Berger, Thomas. *The Christmas Craft Book*, Edinburgh: Floris Books, 1990.

Berger, Thomas and Petra. *The Easter Craft Book*, Edinburgh: Floris Books, 1992.

Carey, Diana and Judy Large. *Festivals, Families and Food*, Gloucestershire, UK: Hawthorn Press, 1982.

Cooper, Stephanie, Christine Fynes-Clinton and Marije Rowling. *The Children's Year*, Gloucestershire, UK: Hawthorn Press, 1986.

Druitt, Ann, Christine Fynes-Clinton and Marije Rowling. *All Year Round*, Gloucestershire, UK: Hawthorn Press, 1997.

Fitzjohn, Sue, Minda Weston and Judy Large. *Festivals Together: A Guide to Multi-Cultural Celebration*, Gloucestershire, UK: Hawthorn Press, 1996.

Jaffke, Freya. *Toymaking with Children*, Edinburgh: Floris Books, 1997.

Leeuwen, M., J. Moeskops and Polly Lawson (Translator). *The Nature Corner: Celebrating the Year's Cycle with a Seasonal Tableau*, Edinburgh: Floris Books, 1990.

Müller, Brunhild. *Painting With Children*, Edinburgh: Floris Books, 1987.

Patterson, Barbara J. and Pamela Bradley. *Beyond the Rainbow Bridge*, Amesbury, MA: Michaelmas Press, 2000.

Petrash, Carol. *Earthways: Simple Environmental Activities for Young Children*, Beltsville, MD: Gryphon House, 1992.

Schmidt, Dagmar and Freya Jaffke. *Magic Wool: Creative Activities with Natural Sheep's Wool*, Edinburgh: Floris Books, 2000.

Vickrey, Anne Einset. *Needle Felting: Art Techniques and Projects*, Geneva, NY: Craft Works Publishing, 2002.

Wolk-Gerche, Angelika and Anna Cardwell (Translator). *More Magic Wool: Creating Figures and Pictures with Dyed Wool*, Edinburgh: Floris Books, 2002.

Resources for Storytelling and Collections of Stories and Puppet Plays

Aulie, Jennifer and Margret Meyerkort. *Spring; Summer; Autumn; Winter; Spindrift;* and *Gateways* (a series of six collections of poems, songs and stories for young children), Stourbridge, UK: Wynstones Press, 1999.

Cole, Joanna (ed.). *Best-Loved Folktales of the World*, Garden City, NY: Doubleday & Company, Inc., 1982.

deForest, Louise (ed.). *Tell Me a Story: Stories from the Waldorf Early Childhood Association of North America*, Spring Valley, NY: Waldorf Early Childhood Association of North America, 2013.

Down, Suzanne. *Around the World With Finger Puppet Animals,* Boulder, CO: 1999.

Down, Suzanne. *Autumn Tales: A Seasonal Collection of Poems and Stories for Early Childhood Teachers and Parents,* and *Spring Tales: A Seasonal Collection of Poems and Stories* Boulder, CO: Storyarts Publications, 2000.

Foster, Nancy. *Let Us Form a Ring: An Acorn Hill Anthology,* and *Dancing As We Sing: Seasonal Circle Plays & Traditional Singing Games,* (1999), Silver Spring, MD: Acorn Hill Children's Center, 1989/1999.

Grimm Brothers. *The Complete Grimm's Fairy Tales*, New York: Pantheon, 1976. (Note: This is an indispensable volume for the kindergarten teacher. Most of these stories are better suited for older children, but "Sweet Porridge" is suitable for a parent/child class.)

Mellon, Nancy. *Storytelling with Children*, Gloucestershire, UK: Hawthorn Press, 2000.

Zahlingen, Bronja. *A Lifetime of Joy*, Spring Valley, NY: Waldorf Early Childhood Association of North America, 2005.

Appendix B

Stories Suitable for a Parent/Child Class

Brown Bear, Brown Bear, What Do You See?

A puppet play for use with a story apron

I began this story apron puppet play, as Connie White did, by singing "The Bear Went Over the Mountain." The bear began the story on my lap, looking about all sides of the "mountain." He would then peek into the first pocket to discover the Bucking Horse. Each successive animal would then peek into the next pocket until all the animals were discovered.

After each animal had made its appearance, I would line them up side-by-side on a small table next to me. When the story was over, each one would slowly return to its pocket, while I hummed "The Bear Went Over the Mountain."

Brown Bear, Brown Bear, what do you see?

I see a bucking horse looking at me.

Bucking Horse, Bucking Horse, what do you see?

I see a wooly lamb looking at me.

Wooly Lamb, Wooly Lamb, what do you see?

I see a mama pig looking at me.

Mama Pig, Mama Pig, what do you see?

I see a white rabbit looking at me.

White Rabbit, White Rabbit, what do you see?

I see a hopping frog looking at me.

Hopping Frog, Hopping Frog, what do you see?

I see a nibble mouse looking at me.

Nibble Mouse, Nibble Mouse, what do you see?

I see a little boy looking at me.

Little Boy, Little Boy, what do you see?

I see a Brown Bear, a Bucking Horse, a Mama Pig, a White Rabbit, a Hopping Frog and a Nibble Mouse all looking at me!

Adapted by Sarah Baldwin, from an adaptation of the Eric Carle story of the same title by Connie White. Could be further adapted depending on the kinds of animal puppets one has.

The Little House

A Russian Folktale

Once upon a time, a peasant was driving a cart full of pots, when one of them fell off and rolled to the ground.

Nibbler-the-Mouse came along, twirling his whiskers and looking at the world. He saw the pot and thought it was as good as a palace. He stood up in front of it and called out:

"Little House, Little House! Who lives in this little house?"

But no one answered, for no one was inside.

"I will live here by myself," said Nibbler-the-Mouse, and in he went and set up house in the pot.

Then along came Croaker-the-Frog. Croak-croak-jump! Croak, croak, jump! When he saw the pot he called:

"Little House, Little House! Who lives in this little house?"

"I do, Nibbler-the-Mouse; and who are you?"

"I am Croaker-the-Frog."

[Mouse:] "Come in and make yourself at home,"

So the Frog jumped in, and the two of them began to live together.

Then a hare came running by. She jumped all around the pot and called out:

"Little House, Little House! Who lives in this little house?"

"I do, Nibbler-the-Mouse."

"I do, Croaker-the-Frog, and who are you?"

"I am Bandy-Legs-the-Hare-the-Hill-Jumper."

[Mouse:] "Come in and make yourself at home."

And the hare jumped in, and the three of them began to live together.

Then a fox came walking by.

"Little House, Little House! Who lives in this little house?"

"I do, Nibbler-the-Mouse."

"I do, Croaker-the-Frog."

"I do, Bandy-Legs-the-Hare-the-Hill-Jumper, and who are you?"

"I am Reynard,-the-Fox-the-Fine-Talker."

[Mouse:] "Come in and make yourself at home."

So the fox went in and the four of them began to live together.

Then a wolf came prowling by and saw the pot.

"Little House, Little House! Who lives in this little house?"

"I do, Nibbler-the-Mouse."

"I do, Croaker-the-Frog."

"I do, Bandylegs-the-Hare-the-Hill-Jumper"

"I do, Reynard-the-Fox-the-Fine-Talker. And who are you?"

"I am Prowler-the-Wolf-who-Lurks-Behind-Bushes."

[Mouse:] "Come in and make yourself at home."

So the wolf went in and the five of them began to live together.

And then there came Bruin-the-Bear. He was very slow and heavy. When he saw the pot, he asked:

"Little House, Little House! Who lives in this little house?"

"I do, Nibbler-the-Mouse."

"I do, Croaker-the-Frog."

"I do, Bandy-Legs-the-Hare-the-Hill-Jumper"

"I do, Reynard-the-Fox-the-Fine-Talker.

"I do, Prowler-the-Wolf-Who-Lurks-Behind-Bushes, and who are you?""

"I am Bruin-the-Bear."

[Mouse:] "Come in and make yourself at home."

And the bear *tried* to climb in with his heavy paws, but the pot broke, and all the animals one-by-one went home again.

First Bruin-the-Bear with his heavy paws.

Then Prowler-the-Wolf-who-Lurks-Behind-Bushes.

Then Reynard-the-Fox-the-Fine-Talker.

Then Bandy-Legs-the-Hare-the-Hill Jumper.

Then Croaker-the-Frog. Croak-croak-jump! Croak-croak-jump!

And at last Nibbler-the-Mouse.

And they all lived happily the rest of their days in their own woodland homes.

[NB: I found it easier to use a basket instead of a pot in this story. I ended with the basket tipping over and all of the animals falling out. A pot could just as easily tip over, without actually "breaking."]

My gratitude to Renate Hiller, handwork teacher at Sunbridge College, for passing on this story.

The Mouse Who Wanted His Tail Back

Once upon a time there was a cat and a mouse. One day they began to play, and then they began to fight. Then the cat stole the mouse's tail!

"Give me my tail back!" said the mouse.

"I will give you back your tail," said the cat, "if you bring me back a bucket of milk."

So the mouse went to the cow.

"Good day, Cow!"

"Good day, Mouse!"

"May I have a bucket of milk?"

"I will give you a bucket of milk if you bring me a bale of hay."

So the mouse went to the farmer.

"Good day, Farmer!"

"Good day, Mouse!"

"May I have a bale of hay?"

"I will give you a bale of hay if you bring me a loaf of bread."

So the mouse went to the baker.

"Good day, Baker!"

"Good day, Mouse!"

"May I have a loaf of bread?"

"You may have a loaf of bread if you will bring me a bag of flour."

So the mouse went to the miller.

"Good day, Miller!"

"Good day, Mouse!"

"May I have a bag of flour?"

"You may have a bag of flour if you promise never to nibble my grain again."

"I promise," said the mouse.

So the miller gave the mouse a bag of flour. The mouse carried the flour the baker.

The baker gave the mouse a loaf of bread. The mouse carried the loaf of bread to the farmer.

The farmer gave the mouse a bale of hay. The mouse carried the bale of hay to the cow.

The cow gave the mouse a bucket of milk. The mouse carried the bucket of milk to the cat.

And the cat gave the mouse his tail back!

Many thanks to Susan Silverio, LifeWays teacher at Spindlewood (a satellite program of Ashwood Waldorf School in Lincolnville, Maine) for this story, which she attributes to Joan Almon.

Stone Soup

A Folktale

There was once a man who had been traveling for a long time. Having run out of food, he was weary and hungry from his journey. When he came upon a small village, he thought, "Maybe someone could share some food with me."

When the man knocked at the door of the first house, he asked the woman who answered, "Could you spare a bit of food? I've traveled a long way and am very hungry."

"I'm sorry, but I have nothing to give you," the woman replied.

So the traveler went to the next door and asked again. The answer was the same. He went from door to door and each time he was turned away.

But then one villager said, "All I have is some water."

"Thank you!" the traveler said smiling gratefully. "We can make some soup from that water. We can make stone soup!"

He asked the woman for a cooking pot and started building a small fire. As the water began to boil, a passing villager stopped and asked him what he was doing. "I'm making stone soup," the traveler replied. "Would you like to join me?"

"First, we must add a special stone," said the traveler. "One with magic in it." He reached into his knapsack and carefully pulled out a special stone he'd been carrying for many years. Then he put it in the simmering pot.

Soon people in the village heard about this strange man who was making soup from a stone. They started gathering around the fire, asking questions. "What does your stone soup taste like?" asked one of the villagers. "Well, it would be better with a few onions," the traveler admitted.

"Oh, I have some onions!" she replied.

Another villager said, "I could bring a few carrots."

Someone else offered, "We still have some potatoes in our garden. I'll go get them!"

One by one, each villager brought something to add to the pot. What had started as just some water and a special stone, had now become a delicious soup—enough to feed the whole village. The traveler and the villagers sat down together to enjoy their feast, and the magic they'd helped to create.

Adapted from a story published by the Stone Soup Foundation: www.journeyofhearts.org/jofh/ kirstimd/soup.htm

The Three Little Kittens

Traditional Nursery Rhyme

The three little kittens they lost their mittens,
And they began to cry,
Oh, mother dear, we sadly fear
That we have lost our mittens.
What! Lost your mittens, you naughty kittens!
Then you shall have no pie.
Mee-ow, mee-ow, mee-ow.
No, you shall have no pie.

The three little kittens they found their mittens,
And they began to cry,
Oh, mother dear, see here, see here,
For we have found our mittens.

Put on your mittens, you silly kittens,
And you shall have some pie.
Purr-r, Purr-r, Purr-r,
Oh let us have some pie.

The three little kittens put on their mittens,
And soon ate up the pie;
Oh, mother dear, we greatly fear
That we have soiled our mittens.
What! Soiled your mittens, you naughty kittens!

Then they began to sigh.

Mee-ow, mee-ow, mee-ow.

Then they began to sigh.

The three little kittens they washed their mittens,

And hung them out to dry;

Oh, mother dear, do you not hear

That we have washed our mittens?

What! Washed your mittens, then you're good kittens,

But I smell a rat close by.

Mee-ow, mee-ow, mee-ow.

We smell a rat close by.

Appears in various collections of nursery rhymes, including The Oxford Dictionary of Nursery Rhymes, *Edited by Iona and Peter Opie (see Bibliography).*

The Turnip

A Folktale

Once upon a time an old man planted a turnip seed and said, "Grow, grow, little turnip, grow sweet! Grow, grow, little turnip, grow strong!"

And the turnip grew up sweet and strong and big and enormous.

Then one day the old man went to pull it up. [SUNG] *He pulled and he tugged and he tugged and he pulled,* but the turnip would not come out.

The old man called the old woman. The old woman pulled on the old man and the old man pulled on the turnip. *They pulled and they tugged and they tugged and they pulled,* but the turnip would not come out.

So the old woman called the child. The child pulled the old woman, the old woman pulled the old man, and the old man pulled on the turnip. *They pulled and they tugged and they tugged and they pulled*, but the turnip would not come out.

So the child called the dog. The dog pulled the child, the child pulled the old woman, the old woman pulled the old man, and the old man pulled on the turnip. *They pulled and they tugged and they tugged and they pulled*, but the turnip would not come out.

So the dog called the cat. The cat pulled the dog, the dog pulled the child, the child pulled the old woman, the old woman pulled the old man, and the old man pulled on the turnip. *They pulled and they tugged and they tugged and they pulled*, but the turnip would not come out.

So the cat called the mouse. The mouse pulled the cat, the cat pulled the dog, the dog pulled the child, the child pulled the old woman, the old woman pulled the old man, and the old man pulled on the turnip. *They pulled and they tugged and they tugged and they pulled . . . They pulled and they tugged and they tugged and they pulled* and OUT popped the most enormous turnip any of them had ever seen!

That night they all had turnip soup for dinner and the little mouse ate the most of all.

Thanks to Beth Vickery, kindergarten teacher at the Cushing Community School in Cushing, Maine, for sharing this version of the popular folktale with me.

Appendix C

Snack Recipes

Birthday Muffins

2 ¼ cups whole wheat pastry flour

3 teaspoons baking powder

1 teaspoon salt

1 cup honey

½ cup oil

½ cup milk + ½ cup milk

1 grated apple (optional)

2 eggs

2 teaspoons vanilla

pinch of cinnamon

Mix dry ingredients. Add honey, oil and ½ cup milk. Beat for two minutes. Add remainder of milk, eggs, cinnamon, vanilla and apple. Beat again. Pour into muffin tins lined with paper. Bake 15-20 minutes at 350°.

Yield: About 20 small muffins or 14 large.

Thanks to Louise deForest, former kindergarten teacher at Green Meadow Waldorf School in Spring Valley, New York, for this recipe.

Very Easy Bread Recipe

1 ½ tablespoons dry yeast

1 cup warm (not boiling) water

dollop of honey

1 stick butter

1 large wooden spoonful of honey

1 tablespoon salt

3 cups warm milk (or warm water)

4-5 cups white flour

4-5 cups whole wheat flour

Optional Ingredients: sunflower seeds, sesame seeds, cinnamon, raisins, millet, rolled oats, nuts, etc.

Preheat oven to 350°. Sprinkle the yeast in a cup of warm water mixed with a dollop of honey. Let the yeast float on top of the water without mixing. Put aside in a warm place until it gets foamy.

Put a stick of butter, the large wooden spoonful of honey and salt in a large bowl. Pour the warm milk (or water) over the butter, honey and salt. When cool enough to hold finger in for a count of 10, add yeast.

Sift in the flour, alternating white and whole wheat, stirring with a wooden spoon to make a sponge. The children love to make it "snow" into the bowl! Add any of the optional "secret ingredients." Cover with a "blanket," and set in a warm place to rest for 10-15 minutes.

Add enough flour to make the dough kneadable. Put a little flour on the table in front of each child, and give each child a small piece of dough to knead. The teacher or parent can knead the majority of the dough so that it will be well-kneaded. As you knead, you can sing:

This is the way we push the dough,
Push the dough, push the dough,
This is the way we push the dough
So early in the morning!

After you've kneaded the dough for 5-10 minutes and it seems very smooth and elastic, gather it together and form into rolls. Place rolls on an oiled baking sheet. If time allows, you could let them rise a little longer on the pan, covered. Bake for about 30 minutes, or until light brown.

Yield: About two loaves.

Thank you, Jill Bieber, former parent/child teacher at Green Meadow Waldorf School, for this much-loved recipe.

Honey Almond Cookies

This is a lovely all-purpose cookie recipe that can be prepared any time of year, and cut out with different shapes of cookie cutters depending on the season. For example, stars at Christmas time or hearts for Valentine's Day. The almonds can be eliminated in case of a nut allergy.

2 sticks butter, softened

$^1/_2$ cup honey

$^3/_4$ teaspoon vanilla extract

$^1/_2$ cup very finely ground almonds

1 cup whole wheat pastry flour

1 cup unbleached white flour

Jam for center of cookies (optional)

With a wooden spoon, cream softened butter, honey and vanilla together until smooth. Add almonds, and then flours. Work in with hands and knead on floured board until well mixed. If there is time, refrigerate dough 1 hour before cutting into shapes.

Roll out the dough approximately $^1/_8$ to $^1/_4$ inch thick on a large floured board or table. (Be generous with the flour: it will save you the frustration of dough stuck to your rolling surface.) Cut into shapes with cutters or an upside-down glass. If filling with jam, have the children make a thumbprint in the center of each cookie and put a dab of jam in it after you place the cookies on a cookie sheet.

Bake on oiled cookie sheets for 7-12 minutes at 325°, depending on cookie size and thickness. (The thinner the cookie, the quicker it bakes.) Bake until the edges of cookies are light brown. Let cool on racks. Both the cookies and dough freeze well.

Yield: 4 to 5 dozen small cookies

Adapted from Horn of the Moon Cookbook by Ginny Callan.

Wholesome Cornbread

2 cups cornmeal

2 cups flour (1 cup whole wheat pastry, 1 cup unbleached white)

3 tablespoons + 1 teaspoon baking powder

$\frac{1}{2}$ teaspoon salt

4 tablespoons sunflower (or other cooking) oil

2 $\frac{1}{2}$ cups water

4 tablespoons blackstrap molasses

2 teaspoons poppy seeds (optional)

Preheat oven to 400°.

In separate bowls, mix together dry ingredients (cornmeal, flour, baking powder and salt) and wet ingredients (oil, water and molasses). Then stir together until moist, adding a bit more water if needed to make a smooth consistency. Pour into two 10-inch oiled glass pie pans and sprinkle top with poppy seeds. Bake 20 minutes. Serve with butter or tahini.

Yield: Two 10-inch loaves; 24 small pieces

Adapted from Horn of the Moon Cookbook by Ginny Callan.

Stone Soup

Onion, garlic or leek

Oil or butter

Water

Vegetable broth powder or cubes

Potatoes (lots)

Carrots (lots)

A clean, washed stone

Optional:

Tamari

Herb salt

Beets, squash, sweet potato, barley, rice, dried beans, green beans, peas, etc.

Soak any beans or grains overnight.

Sauté in butter or oil, a small amount of onion, garlic or leek in a large stockpot. Add as much water as needed to suit the size of your group. Add the appropriate amount of vegetable broth. Add the soaked and rinsed beans or grains, if you choose. Season with tamari and herb salt, if desired.

While the broth is simmering, adults and children can work together to cut the vegetables into bite-sized pieces. Give young children small pieces to chop with a butter knife or a "crinkle cutter" (a wonderful utensil used to make crinkle-cut potatoes, that is not sharp). It is nice to have small cutting boards for each child.

Add vegetables and simmer until all are tender.

When the soup was ready to be served, I would secretly put the stone (big enough to eliminate any choking hazard) in the bottom of one child's bowl. The children would anticipate in excitement finding the "magic wishing stone" in their bowl. After the stone was found, it was then wiped off, held carefully in hand while the child who found it made a wish. The stone was then passed round the table for all (adults and children) to wish upon.

Thanks to Connie Manson for passing on the tradition of the "wishing stone."

Appendix D

Sample Letter Sent to New Parents in Parent/Child Program

Dear _____ ,

Welcome to Ashwood Waldorf School! I am delighted that you and your child will be joining the Parent/Child Program and hope your experience will be a positive and enriching one. I would like to go over some of the details of the program, so you will know what to expect when you join us for the first time.

Our meetings take place in "Rosewood" (the Early Childhood Center), all the way up the hill at the Ashwood School. There are three classrooms in the building—ours is the door to the far right as you enter the building.

Slippers

Please bring a pair of slippers or warm socks for you and your child to wear in class. This not only protects our wood floors, but also helps to create the peaceful mood we strive for in the classroom.

Parking

The school has asked that no one park at the top of the hill between 10:00 a.m. and 3:00 p.m., because the grade-schoolers use that area for games. This means that you will need to park in the grade school parking lot (the circular lot at the bottom of the hill), and walk up. A walk in the morning is wonderful for young children, and you may want to allow an extra five minutes or so on the morning of your class to allow for a leisurely stroll.

Rhythm of the Morning

Our mornings together will begin at 9:15 a.m. with children playing freely in the classroom while the adults are engaged with housekeeping activities, snack preparation or a simple craft project (all snacks and craft materials will be provided). Often the children will wish to help with these activities. At about 10:15 a.m. we will clean up, set the table, then have a circle time during which we'll learn some seasonal songs, nursery rhymes, finger plays and simple games.

We will then wash hands, sit down at our table, light a candle, and say a blessing thanking the earth for our food. Then we share a snack together, which usually consists of organic whole grains, fruits and vegetables. We sweeten only with honey or maple syrup. (Please let me know if your child has any food sensitivities so that I may plan snacks accordingly.) After we've cleaned up the snack table and washed the dishes, we will end our morning with a short story or puppet play before singing our goodbye song. You are then free to play outdoors for as long as you'd like.

There are a few important things to keep in mind before your first class. First, since young children are such creatures of imitation, it is best for the adults to be engaged in calm, purposeful activity. Mending, knitting, sewing, washing, ironing, sweeping, repairing toys, etc. are all good activities for us to be involved in while the children explore the room, ride the rocking horse, play in the kitchen, take care of the babies, and so on. It's best to keep conversation to a minimum—both with adults and with the children—so that the children can become more deeply engaged with their play. Play is the young child's work and the best environment for encouraging the development of their imaginations is a calm room, humming with busy, purposeful activity—without too much adult chatting.

At each class there will be napkins to wash on a scrub board, sweeping and ironing to be done, cutting boards to be waxed, grain to be ground with the stone grinder, etc. I ask that each parent try to engage themselves in at least one of these tasks per morning. Why, you may wonder, are you being asked to perform these domestic activities (many of which we don't even do at home!) after paying to join this class? We do this to provide an example to the child that is worthy of imitation—an individual engaged in calm, productive activity—bringing focus, care and attention to the task at hand. The atmosphere created by adults engaged in such purposeful activity creates a protective and nurturing environment for the child in which he can either help with the chores, or explore the room confidently on his own.

Parent Evenings

We will have time for adult conversation and discussion during scheduled parent evenings. There will be at least one such evening during each session. At these meetings, we will address issues such as creative discipline, creating healthy rhythms at home, sleep and mealtimes, the effect of television on the young child, etc. There will be time at each meeting for your questions about what we are doing in class, or parenting concerns you may have.

Settling Conflicts

I have found that it is best when each parent remains aware of and takes responsibility for his or her own child. It is important to remember that one- to four-year-olds are just beginning to learn social graces, and most simply cannot share yet. They will learn in time, but what we do is much more important than what we say at this age. Simply saying, "Madison is riding the horse right now," and taking Lizzy away to the play kitchen to make muffins, works much better than trying to explain the concept of taking turns, while Madison screams and Lizzy hits her and tries to wrestle the rocking horse away. Redirecting in this way is not always easy, especially in a group, but it gets easier with practice. Together we can help one another.

One more request I would make is that if your child does something to disrupt a group activity (for instance, grabs a puppet during the puppet play or is disruptive during circle time), first of all relax and know that this is normal toddler behavior. But remember that it is your responsibility to promptly redirect your child. It may be necessary to take her out of the room for a few minutes. This prevents the teacher from having to interrupt the flow of the activity in order to deal with the situation.

Lastly, don't despair if your child does not want to join the circle or participate in other group activities. Again, this is perfectly normal. Some children will join the group only after observing for several weeks, and some will never join in during the course of the session. This is fine. It is important to know that even if a child seems to be busily occupied in another part of the room, he is very often participating inwardly. In his own mind, he is fully a part of the group. I can't tell you how many times a parent has told me of a child who never participated in the circle in class, but who, upon getting into the car to go home, would sing every song and repeat every story word-for-word! Always invite the child to join the group, but please don't feel any pressure to have your child join in if he clearly is not ready to. The only thing I ask is that if your child chooses not to join the circle, please stay with your child wherever he is in the room. It can be helpful to be near your child, but to focus your attention on the circle.

Rhythm and Repetition

You will be hearing these words often! Very young children delight in and are nurtured by familiarity. Knowing what to expect and what comes next gives them a healthy sense of security. For this reason, we repeat the same songs, rhymes and stories—some for an entire session. It may inspire boredom after a while in us as adults, but children under five never seem to tire of hearing the same songs and stories over and over again. As they begin to learn songs by heart and sing along, they gain confidence in their abilities. Each time they hear a story, it goes deeper and deeper to the inner core of their being, becoming part of them. So please trust that the repetition you experience in class is done out of a conscious desire to meet the needs of the child, and is not due to the teacher's lack of repertoire!

Finally, remember that consistency is extremely important for young children. Please try your best to make it to every class (unless, of course, your child is sick!), and try to be on time. It is very hard for little ones to settle into the rhythm of the morning if they are not experiencing the whole day from the beginning.

Snow Days

If the weather is questionable, please listen to 102.5 FM for school cancellation announcements. If Camden/Rockport schools (SAD 28) are closed, then Ashwood will be closed as well and the Parent/Child class will not meet. We will either arrange for a make-up class or offer you a credit for the missed class.

If you have any questions or concerns, please do not hesitate to call me at home. I welcome hearing your concerns and questions. I look forward to meeting you and your child!

Warmly,

"Miss Sarah"

P.S. All parents new to the program will be receiving a copy of *Beyond the Rainbow Bridge: Nurturing Our Children from Birth to Seven*. This book is an excellent introduction to the Waldorf approach to parenting and early childhood education. Another highly recommended book is *You Are Your Child's First Teacher*, by Rahima Baldwin Dancy, which is more comprehensive. I will have a copy to lend as well as a number of other books related to parenting, child development and Waldorf education. Because of the limited number of volumes I have to lend, I ask that parents borrow only one book at a time. Books can also be ordered through the school if you are interested in purchasing a copy.

Appendix E

Sample Fliers for Publicizing a Parent/Child Program

PARENT/CHILD
PROGRAM

A gentle & nurturing environment for children one to four years old
accompanied by a parent or caregiver

Sessions are 9:15–11:15 one or more mornings per week for ten weeks at Ashwood's
Early Childhood Center in Rockport. Led by a Waldorf-trained, early childhood educator.

The morning includes:

Creative free play • Snack preparation • Handcrafts
Morning circle • Snack • Story • Outdoor play

Ashwood Waldorf School

Early Childhood through Grade 8 • 180 Park Street • Rockport, Maine
For more information or to enroll, call 236-8021

PARENT/CHILD PROGRAM

Ashwood Waldorf School

The Parent/Child program offers a gentle and nurturing environment for children ages 1½–3½ years old accompanied by a parent or caregiver.

*T*HE MORNING BEGINS with creative play. The children might create houses, castles, or caves with colored gauze sheets draped over wooden play frames. Around these structures, they may use items gathered from nature, hobbyhorses, cloth crowns and silk capes, as tools of their rich imaginations. Still others might choose to play with the handknit farm animals, felt rabbits, or cloth dolls. The blocks are organic shapes made from pieces of tree limbs sanded smooth.

Children include parents in their play according to their fluctuating needs. Those parents not engaged in child-led play may work on a simple craft project provided by the teacher, or help with snack preparation. Group circle activities delight the children through much repetition of seasonal songs, nursery rhymes and finger plays. Snacks consist of nutritious whole foods that the children help to prepare.

A story is told with the aid of bits of branches, woolen animals, and handmade people all placed on cloths draped to create a natural scene. Stories are repeated throughout the session in acknowledgement of young children's developmental need for and pleasure in repetition. They are generally chosen to reflect the current cycle of nature.

The morning ends with unstructured outdoor play. Each week the same flow of activities takes place so that even the youngest children experience the morning routine and begin to participate as part of the larger group.

Sessions are 9:00-11:00AM one morning per week, for six to ten weeks. Due to the increasing popularity of this program, two separate sessions are being offered on Thursday and Friday mornings for the '99-'00 school year. Classes are led by Sarah Baldwin, a Waldorf-trained early childhood educator. Cost for a six-week session is $90. For more information or to enroll in the Winter or Spring session, contact Maureen Egan, Admissions Director.

Ashwood Waldorf School
Early Childhood through Grade 8 • Park Street • Rockport, Maine • 207.236.8021

Appendix F

Lifeways Principles and Practices

Lifeways Principles for Caring for Young Children

1. Children thrive in the presence of devoted caregivers who enjoy life and caring for children. This is the foundation for learning and healthy development. Young children learn primarily through imitation/empathy and, therefore, need to be cared for by people with integrity and warmth who are worthy of being imitated.

2. Having consistent caregivers (over several years) is essential for young children, especially from birth to three years old and, preferably, up to primary school age.

3. In infancy and early childhood, daily life experience is the "curriculum." The child's relationships to the caregivers and to the environment are the two most important aspects through which the child can experience healthy life rhythms/routines. These include rest and play, regular meal times, exploring nature, practical/domestic activities, social creativity, music and simple artistic activities.

4. Childhood is a valid and authentic time unto itself and not just a preparation for schooling.

5. Infants and toddlers develop most healthily when allowed to have freedom of movement in a safe environment.

6. Children need relationship to people of all ages and can both give and receive special blessing when in the company of elders and youth who enjoy children. Infants and toddlers thrive in family-style blended-age care.

7. Young children thrive in a home-like environment that offers beauty, comfort and security. Healthy sense development is fostered when most of their clothing and playthings are of non-synthetic materials and their toys allow for open-ended, imaginative play.

8. Caregivers need an environment where they can create an atmosphere of "home," where they can build true relationship to the children in their care, and where they can feel autonomous and appreciated.

9. Each child carries an intrinsic value and is gifted with purpose. No child is an "accident."

10. Caregivers also have an intrinsic purpose and need to be recognized and appropriately compensated for the value of their work, which lays the foundation of life-long learning for children in their care.

11. Human relationship, rather than technology, is the essential tool for teaching the young child all foundational skills for life.

12. Parents of young children thrive in a care setting where they are loved, respected and helped to feel love and understanding for their children.

LifeWays Suggested Basic Practices in the Care of Young Children at Home and in Child Care

General

*   LifeWays practices are based upon the fundamental need for relationship-based care (bonding and continuity), neurological research, and recognition of living arts (domestic, nurturing, creative and social arts) as central to the advancement of children's social, emotional and intellectual skills. These practices can be applied in parenting, in family childcare homes, and in childcare centers.

*   In child care, "suites" consist of small groups of children who stay together with the same caregivers over a several-year period, creating a more homelike atmosphere and better teacher–child ratios.

*   Emphasis is placed on practical life skills such as building, gardening, cleaning, cooking, washing, repairing, and sewing, among other things.

*   Movement/play curriculum emphasizes child-initiated activities that promote healthy musculoskeletal development, providing opportunities for unstructured, spontaneous movement in a safe environment. Traditional games and finger-plays provide opportunities for the children to imitate healthy movement, develop proprioception and increase both their small and large motor skills.

* The children go outside in all but the most inclement weather. This helps them become more robust and strengthens their bond with the environment in which they live. A protected area is provided for crawlers and infants. Where it is possible, infants who fall asleep outside can remain outside, snuggly wrapped and covered in a buggy, until time to go in. Fresh air provides a deep, more restful sleep.

* Emphasis is on loving human interaction with warm speech, live singing, verses, and stories rather than technology. LifeWays Centers and Childcare Homes are television- and video-free environments except for use in administration and adult education.

* Child guidance is based on the L.O.V.E. Approach to Discipline which includes Listening, Laughter, Order, Objectivity, Versatility, Vulnerability, Energy, and Enthusiasm.

* Foundation for lifelong literacy is fostered through storytelling and puppetry, individual lap time with a book, through poetry, verse, and music on a daily basis, through drama, and through the daily interactions of play and movement in a healthy, secure environment.

* Pre-School/Kindergarten program is a developmentally appropriate, play-based approach found in Waldorf preschools and kindergartens throughout the world.

* We provide the best in natural organic foods (whenever this is possible) and involve the children in the food preparation.

* Festivals and celebrations honoring the various cultural backgrounds of the families, as well as traditional seasonal festivals and birthday parties, are offered.

* When possible, ongoing relationships are established with senior adults and youth who visit on a regular basis.

* Foreign language-community friends who speak a native language other than English may be invited to play simple games or sing simple songs with the children on a routine basis.

Specific to the Infants (in addition to the applicable points above)

∗   Infants are provided safe environments in which to explore and move freely—no walkers, bouncers, infant gyms, or other mechanical devices are necessary.

∗   The infants are carefully wrapped for sleeping to provide a healthy sense of security and warmth, and caps are provided to protect their sensitive heads and ears.

∗   Rocking and cuddling are encouraged to develop a healthy sense of touch and movement and to promote security, bonding, and comfort.

∗   Diaper-changing is a special time for connecting with the caregiver and may include a special name song for the baby, or a simple nursery rhyme, and a gentle massage. The baby will be encouraged to participate in clothing herself or himself; for example, by learning to lift its own bottom for diapering or pulling on its own socks when capable.

∗   Clear, articulate, melodic speech is expected of the caregivers, who are also encouraged to speak frequently to the infants throughout the day.

LifeWays North America
lifewaysnorthamerica.org

Made in the USA
Coppell, TX
16 July 2021